W9-BUT-151

Fascism

Revolutions of Our Time

Fascism

Otto-Ernst Schüddekopf

Metropolitan State University
Library Services
St. Paul, MN 55106

Praeger Publishers
New York · Washington

BOOKS THAT MATTER
Published in the United States of
America in 1973 by
Praeger Publishers, Inc.,
111 Fourth Avenue, New York,
N.Y. 10003

© 1973 by Otto-Ernst Schüddekopf

All rights reserved

No part of this publication may be
reproduced, stored in a retrieval system
or transmitted in any form or by any
means, electronic, mechanical,
photocopying, recording or otherwise,
without the prior permission of the
Copyright owner.

Library of Congress Catalog Card
Number: 72-93189

Printed in Great Britain

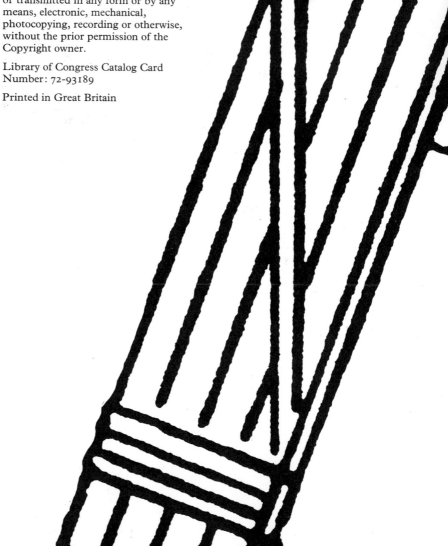

Contents

Foreword

The left and the right, in political terms, just as the apathetic centre, represent those who have descended from the plateau on which the historically active man stands, he who is both conservative and revolutionary, and does not see these correlatives as isolated phenomena.
HEIMITO VON DODERER

The British historian Geoffrey Barraclough in his *Guide to Imperialism* (1969) compared the concept and the practice of 'imperialism' to a chameleon. Nevertheless, there is no doubt that this phenomenon has existed. The same is true of fascism: opinions in the academic and political world differ widely over what it was and is. What is beyond doubt is that the movement was of great historical importance and that it was the cause of the worst war that humanity has yet experienced.

It would be impossible to see and describe the history of fascism throughout Europe and the world as a historical-political system from its very beginning until the present day, and no one has yet attempted to do so. Those who were dissatisfied – and rightly so – with isolated studies of different nations, turned to the sociological method of constructing 'patterns and models' in order to assess historical reality. Both these 'guide-lines' are useful but, if used in isolation, they may lead to distortions.

I shall therefore attempt to combine both methods, as more and more historians are doing today. I shall use a socio-economic cross-section analysis together with a historical depth-analysis. This seems to me the only possible way to produce a readable and satisfying treatment of the subject, in view of the present state of research in this field. Thus, the conflicting forces within fascism, and its conflict with the world surrounding it, become the history of fascism.

At the International Conference of Historians held in Moscow in 1970 the Hungarian historian Miclos Lackó gave a lecture on fascism in Eastern Central Europe, which provoked a lively discussion. He too argued that, following the period of individual historical examination, the time had now come for the typological approach. He stressed, however, that neither method is satisfactory if used alone: the necessary synthesis would still be lacking. Because of the enormous differences between the varying kinds of fascism, Lackó confined himself to the analysis of a particular region within Europe. This method is useful and stimulating, and I shall make use of it in the following study to attempt to combine historical, sociological and geographical approaches in order to treat the phenomenon of fascism in its totality.

Preconditions of fascism

It is generally assumed, though some disagree, that the crisis-prone nature of modern society in the first half of the twentieth century was responsible for the growth of fascism. Ernst Nolte, distinguished for his research into the subject, said that 'the liberal system' was a pre-condition of fascism. By this he meant the structural weaknesses within the parliamentary democracies of many European states after 1918. He sees fascism as the European bourgeoisie's response to the challenge of bolshevism, which was itself based on the last European faith, Marxism.

This interpretation is by no means as new as many might think today. In 1931 a distinguished left-wing jurist, Hermann Heller, had spoken of the political crisis in Europe, and had pointed out that the experiment in 'mass social democracy' did not seem to be succeeding. In his view, society, shaken to its roots by bourgeois and proletarian revolutions, had lost faith in it. All traditional values, including those of religion, had become meaningless and the 'community of political values' within Europe had disappeared. Influential German jurists such as Laband, Jellinek and Kelsen referred to the concept of democracy as society without a leader. Culture too, according to Heller, was being shaken to its very foundations. Thus cultural and historical criticism, deep-seated fear of the decadence of modern society, and the growing *fin-de-siècle* atmosphere in bourgeois intellectual circles all provided fertile ground for the seeds of fascism. For the bourgeoisie the 'true' ideologies, to use Hegel's term, had been 'emptied' of their content, and so it sought for an *ersatz* (substitute) ideology which it found in fascism, particularly where the will to

The architects of the Treaty of Versailles, Lloyd George, Orlando, Clemenceau and Wilson, after the signing in 1919. The terms, branding Germany exclusively responsible for World War I, and allocating some of her territories to her neighbours, paved the way for the later catastrophe.

create a constitutional state had become weakened. Bourgeois liberalism, which in 1918 had triumphed, formally at least, over the traditional monarchical powers, was even then, according to the historian Hugh Trevor-Roper, diseased at the roots and capable neither of rebuilding a society shattered by the war nor of resisting attacks by the left and the right. Thus the fascist march on Rome in 1922 went, in the words of Bernard Shaw in 1928, 'through the indignant liberal opposition like a red hot poker through a pound of butter'. Contemporary historians seem generally to have thought that society after 1918 was sick, and not only in Germany. Though neither Hitler nor the Second World War nor Auschwitz need have happened it was obvious that Italian and German democracy were doomed. Therefore, the question of whether the fascist take-overs in Italy and Germany in 1922 and 1933 were legal, or *coups d'état*, or revolutions, seems irrelevant. The internal political conflicts in these states had become so violent that a balance of power in the traditional manner of parliamentary democracies no longer seemed possible.

If the crisis within modern European society had only been partial, limited solutions might have been found, such as the National Government in Great Britain, Daladier's dictatorial government in France, and Roosevelt's New Deal in the United States of America. But the crisis affected the lives of the people at almost all levels; whether victor or vanquished, whether as a result of oppressive peace conditions, loss of territory, gains that were too small, with the resulting over-population, the *malaise* affecting the bourgeois middle classes, the vivid experience of *Volksgemeinschaft*, or *collettività* – comradeship of the kind experienced in the trenches during the war, which people wanted to keep in the post-war period – and finally the economic and financial crises within the affected states. These factors created discontented masses outside parliament and caused the ruling classes to decide that it might perhaps be advisable for the fascists to participate in their government. The fact that this limited participation led to totalitarian regimes was due to the fascist leaders' infinite desire for power, and the conservative and liberal ruling classes' over-estimation of their own strength.

The dream had become a nightmare.
                    GEORGE L. MOSSE

Eras of fascism

Present-day historians, following the example of Ernst Nolte, refer to fascism as 'the characteristic political trend' of the 1918 to 1945 period, the era of the World Wars. This judgement is valid for the obvious reason that fascism did not exist as a significant political movement before 1918, while it rose to power in two major European nations after that date. But it is also valid for another reason, namely, that the phenomenon of fascism dictated

A delegation of the Finnish Lappo movement after talks with the Finnish Foreign Minister. This independent nationalist movement almost succeeded in coming to power at the beginning of the 1930s. It was a party which arose of its own accord and not as the result of external forces.

the terms of political combat in this period: if fascism was in part a response to the apparent challenge of communism, it is also the case that the communist (as well as the socialist and liberal) parties found their inter-war significance in the struggle to resist this new movement.

The early communist analyses of fascism clearly recognized its epoch-making character. At the Fourth Congress of the Communist International, Zinoviev referred to 'the era of fascism'. His interpretations and those of Karl Radek and Clara Zetkin showed a high degree of objectivity and pointed out clearly the mistakes made by socialist and communist workers' movements. In 1928 the Italian socialist Filippo Turati saw the germs of fascism spreading to every capitalist country and considered it possible that the whole of Europe might become fascist. In 1931 the Belgian socialist Hendrik Man commented that an anti-proletarian 'white-collar proletariat', the so-called 'new middle class', had grown up all over Europe together with the growth of fascist mass movements. In 1934 the historian Arthur Rosenberg, who had left Germany in 1933, spoke of the 'fascist world sickness'. A book published in 1936 names forty-nine fascist movements in twenty European countries and another published after 1945 mentions twenty-three states which had fascist movements during the era after 1923. The numerical insignificance of most of these movements makes it impossible to use them as a basis for assuming the concept of a fascist era, although they achieved power in more than a few states – in Italy from 1922 to 1943, in Germany from 1933 to 1945, in Rumania under General Antonescu from 1940 to 1941, in Croatia under Ante Pavelić's Ustasha regime from 1941 to 1945. In Finland, the fascist Lappo movement nearly won power at the beginning of the 1930s, particularly as there it was an independent national movement which arose at first of its own accord and not as the result of external forces.

The antecedents of fascism can be traced back

The *Action Française* movement was born of and acquired maturity, during the Dreyfus Affair, its influence waned during the twenties but made itself felt in the thirties, profiting from the triumph of other European fascist movements. During the occupation it collaborated with the Germans.

The *Führer* and the *Duce* at a rally of young Italian fascists near Rome. Italian fascism in its first decade failed to acquire either the total power or the racialist characteristics that the National Socialist regime assumed in only a few years.

into the nineteenth century and earlier, as we shall see; but the history of fascism as an effective political movement began only with the organization of the Italian fascists in 1919 and the founding of the National Socialist German Workers' Party (NSDAP) by Adolf Hitler in the following year. As Italian fascism in its first decade failed to acquire either the total power or the radical characteristics that the National Socialist regime assumed in only a few years, it can safely be said that the imperialist era of fascism began in Europe in 1935. Italy, following in the wake of the Third Reich, turned to political expansion abroad and at the same time fascist movements sprang up in many European countries, all closely modelled on the German movement. Influenced by a world economic crisis and by the existence of the two fascist powers, the east European

dictatorships began to change into fascist regimes, and even in the old democracies such as Switzerland strong fascist fronts began to form. Fifty per cent of all European fascist movements developed after 1933, such as those in Norway and in the Netherlands. Their leaders, like Vidkun Quisling or Anton Adriaan Mussert, saw Adolf Hitler's take-over of power as the beginning of a new era in European history. Even Mussolini admitted in 1943, when he had fallen from power, that 'everything went well until 1937': it would have been better had he died then.

Their finest hour and the preparations for their inglorious end began for the many leaders of the small fascist movements throughout Europe with the outbreak of war in 1939. The Germans recognized them as the only political power in their countries,

The imperialist era of fascism began in Europe in 1935, and Italy, following in the wake of the Third Reich, turned to political expansion abroad. Here, Italian motorised troops advance into Abyssinia, a campaign which resulted in triumph for Mussolini in 1936.

Metropolitan State University
Library Services

but in return they completely lost their independence, and became mere lackeys. Only with the war against Russia did this conglomeration of heterogeneous fascist movements, which were lacking in unity and often mutually hostile, acquire a single aim and ideology – the battle to save Europe from bolshevism. The *Waffen-SS* (the SS military formation) provided them with both: from then on they were concerned with the 'future and fate of western Europe' and 'the awareness of western *Schicksalsgemeinschaft* (common destiny)'. In western democracies such as Great Britain and the United States of America, fascist groups sank into insignificance after 1938 once their countries had turned against the fascist powers.

Fascism saw itself as an epoch-making force: Mussolini reckoned with a fascist era lasting about sixty years from his take-over of power in 1922. Later, he expected his regime to determine the future of the twentieth century, just as in Hungary Julius Gömbös, the half-fascist Prime Minister from 1932 to 1936, thought he could determine the future of his country for the next century. In September 1934 Hitler declared at Nuremberg: 'There will be no more revolutions in Germany for the next thousand years.' The thousand-year Reich as an aim had begun. But the war, which was the breath of life itself to fascism, ultimately brought about its defeat and its end as an era in Europe.

The concept of fascism

Theories of fascism were being developed even before Mussolini came to power. But the further we get from the so-called era of fascism, the less 'objective' the theories become. If we analyse all these theories and examine all the varieties of fascism in order to get a clear picture of it as a historical phenomenon, then it becomes clear that there can be no single all-embracing definition, at least, not in our time. The main reason for this is that the different fascisms were eclectic in their practical aims and doctrines. They borrowed whatever suited them from other political doctrines: Mussolini took the form and content of his movement from d'Annunzio, who in turn had used various ingredients to make his brew; Hitler was inspired largely by the Bohemian and Austrian National Socialist movement before 1914; the Falange leader, José Antonio Primo de Rivera, tried to copy the British fascist leader, Sir Oswald Mosley; the doctrines and programmes of the small fascist movements throughout northern and western Europe were mostly imitations of Italian or German fascism.

If we take the concept of 'fascism' in its strictest sense, it can only be applied to Italy. The term itself is of Italian origin, and Mussolini chose to define it specifically as a movement founded by him in Italy.

Mussolini with the nationalist poet, d'Annunzio, who added an intellectual and poetic dimension to the fascist movement. His expressionist poems were a celebration of the lust for conquest.

Right: Antonio Primo de Rivera, the Falange leader, addressing the second national congress of the Falange at Madrid in 1935. He styled himself on the British fascist leader, Sir Oswald Mosley, and his doctrines and programmes were mostly imitations of Italian or German fascism.

Below: This pamphlet was in the form of a dialogue between Hitler and his poet and journalist friend, Dietrich Eckart. Eckart, who was one of the founders of the Nazi party had considerable influence on Hitler's thinking. His magazine *Auf gut Deutsch* promulgated anti-semitic and *völkisch* ideas.

Der

Bolschewismus

von Moses
bis Lenin

Zwiegespräch
zwischen

Adolf Hitler
und mir

Von

Dietrich Eckart †

Hoheneichen-Verlag München, Hildegardstraße 9

Italy too was the country in which the fundamental fascist socio-economic system of corporatism was most firmly implanted. On the other hand, Italian fascism lacked some of those elements which, as we shall see, characterized other obviously fascist movements in Europe. The attempt to identify these various elements and to assess their significance for the different national movements should not be taken so far that it obscures the common features which allow us to speak of 'fascism' as an identifiable historical phenomenon. Fascism is elusive, because its ideologies were ill-defined, consisting in part of no more than large generalizations capable of infinitely varying interpretations. The doctrines of the separate European movements were frequently self-contradictory as well as being mutually inconsistent. Moreover, another distorting factor is the unequal success of the several movements: because fascism itself acknowledged an intimate link between programme and practice – expressed in the dedication to violent activism, or in the emphasis on the word 'movement' as a synonym for dynamic energy as well as for political party – there is a danger of overemphasizing one or other element in fascism merely because of its realization in those countries where fascist parties came to power.

Communist interpretations were, as I have already said, very realistic. Early on there were warnings of the danger of the 'German fascists', but by the early 1920s they were rashly anticipating that fascism would destroy capitalism and allow the communists to take over. In 1924 Stalin spoke of the 'social fascism' of the social democrat movements in Europe: 'Fascism is a fighting organization of the bourgeoisie and relies on the active support of the

Sir Oswald Mosley wearing the black-shirt uniform of the British fascists. After fascist-provoked street fighting, particularly in London's East End, the Public Order Act of 1937 banned the wearing of party uniforms.

social democrats.' This thesis formed official communist doctrine after 1928–9, apart from the brief episode of the Popular Front government in France. Even the events of 1933 did nothing to change this. Anyone in Europe who was politically active and not a loyal communist party member was declared a fascist. The Italian communists who had emigrated to Moscow urged Moscow and the Comintern in vain not to tar everything with the same fascist brush. Even an intelligent man like the Marxist August Thalheimer wrote that the final phase of fascist development had begun when the bourgeoisie, in order to save its social position, gave up its political one. But that had already happened in Prussian Germany in 1864–6. Any objective analysis must take fully into account the similarities and the differences between the individual fascist movements, for one thing is certain: there is no such thing as *the* fascist movement or ideology. However,

Chancellor Engelbert Dollfuss, an exponent of Austrian clerical-fascism, opposed Nazi Germany's desire to incorporate Austria into the Reich. He was assassinated in the abortive Nazi *coup d'état* of July 1934.

the attempt to describe and classify all the varieties of fascism has given rise to a bewildering number of subdivisions within the general category, with labels such as radical fascism, clerico-fascism, left-wing fascism, proto-fascism, fascistoid, and so on. These and the many other terms that derive from the initial concept are not very helpful in practice, unless we have first established a comprehensive definition, providing a fixed point against which all the micro-definitions can be measured. To subdivide without having identified this comprehensive category is to put the cart before the horse; on the other hand, it is clear that an examination of the individual national movements will contribute the information with which to modify or extend the primary concept. Thus the relationship between an 'ideal' fascism and the actual historical varieties is mutually conditioning. The historian must resist the temptation to define the term out of existence by subjecting it

Lenin and Stalin in Gorki, in 1922. In April of that year Stalin became the Central Committee's first secretary-general and although belonging to the Communist party's top leadership, was comparatively unknown outside the party circle.

The leaders of the earlier, milder forms of fascist or authoritarian governments were: Professor Salazar, president of Portugal, seated on the left, (**above**) . . .

. . . and (**right**) Marshal Pilsudski, the Polish dictator, seen here with Josef Beck, the Polish Foreign Minister, and, centre, Goebbels, the German Minister of propaganda.

Above right: Edouard Daladier, the French Prime Minister, who after signing the appeasing Munich agreement in September 1938, lost his support from the left and up to the outbreak of war had increasingly to rely on the right.

to an over-pedantic critique; but at the same time he must be equally on his guard against ignoring the genuine differences between one national type and another, or accepting as real the superficial resemblances between them. Neither an indiscriminate use of the term – as in the current pejorative attribution 'social fascist' to manipulative, non-Marxist mass movements – nor an exaggeratedly exclusive restriction of its application will help in the task of identifying the nature and origins of this European phenomenon. We shall give due weight to the problems when we come to investigate the

elements and driving forces of fascism.

We can also approach the typology of fascism from the geographical, regional point of view. Lackó, whom we have already mentioned, suggests a division into three: one region covering those countries under advanced capitalism, one covering those economically underdeveloped countries such as Bulgaria, Serbia, Slovakia and Greece, and one covering the east central European countries. The latter includes countries with very different economic systems, such as Austria, Czechoslovakia, Poland, Hungary and Rumania. There is a clear downward gradient from the west through central to eastern Europe, and this would favour the division into three. Nolte, however, prefers a division into four: the Balkans and south-eastern Europe, eastern Europe and the Baltic provinces, central Europe, and finally western Europe and Scandinavia. But generally the division into three would seem more useful.

Before attempting a socio-historical examination of fascism and its elements, a few examples of each region should be examined historically, using Lackó's regional divisions. We will proceed from west to east, following the gradient of social development.

In France just before the turn of the century, in the wake of the Dreyfus affair, a new form of political activity began to develop outside the framework of the elite parties, composed principally of local dignitaries and notables, and representing provincial and sectional, rather than national and common, interests. The modern mass movements were beginning to form – first came the league (*ligue, liga, Bund*), an organization which was activist, yet had a hierarchical structure, resembling a secret or religious order. The nationalist and monarchist *Ligue de la Patrie Française*, and the *Action Française* which came after it in 1898–9, were both completely reactionary in their ideology. They wanted to recreate France as it had been before 1789 – something the later fascists were not in the least interested in. However, it is beyond doubt that these leagues did have many fascist elements, and that they were thus the forerunners of fascism. For them *raison*

Charles Maurras the most brilliant intellectual among the anti-republican, anti-German, anti-semitic activists of the *Action Française*.

d'état was identical with national interest – thus they shared the National Socialist thesis that the people's good was the highest law.

This *nationalisme intégral* – lacking all Jacobin concessions to the higher community of mankind – regarded the ideas of 1789 as 'Germanic poison', as did the radical Italian fascists later on. There were close practical and theoretical ties with French syndicalism. The movement wanted not only to reintroduce the monarchy, but to abolish parliamentary democracy totally. The relationship to the theories of the syndicalist Georges Sorel is unmistakable.

The *Action Française* had many elements in it that were later to be found in fascism, but it was never called fascist, perhaps because it never came to power, and because it was superseded by even more radical groups. These elements included their

Metropolitan State University
Library Services
St. Paul, MN 55106

A French communist party demonstration opposed by the *Croix de Feu* — a para-military proto-fascist organization. It was originally an ex-serviceman's league of highly decorated veterans but it later accepted all 'patriotically minded' citizens and its membership rose to more than a quarter of a million by 1936. It was dissolved by the Popular Front government under Léon Blum.

concept of the nation, their rejection of all parliamentary activity, the organization of a militant minority, the *Féderation National des Camelots du Roi* (the king's street urchins) which organized the street battles, and the aim of national revolution which would lead them to power, for until then they had been but a state within a state.

It was, however, the *Action Française*, whose political influence began to decline after 1923, which was the actual parent of French fascism in ideological and practical terms. It provided many of the ideas which were later radicalized, and out of it grew the *cadres*, small activist groups of French fascists. These movements, which were 'wide-spread and complex', were at their most active and successful from 1933 to 1944. The many political and economic scandals and the many changes in government had shattered the stability of the republic. This instability led to the rebellion of the discontented middle classes on 6 February 1934, and the fall of Daladier's government. The Popular Front was formed as a counter-movement and won a decisive victory in the elections of 1936.

The various para-military organizations, in so

far as they were not run in accordance with purely French principles, tended to follow the Italian example, particularly Marcel Bucard's 'Francists' who were really fascists. The three main groups were Pierre Taittinger's *Jeunesses Patriotes*, the Bonapartist and anti-Semitic *Solidarité Française*, and the *Croix de Feu* (Cross of Fire) which was the strongest group, composed of former officers led by Colonel de la Roque. Their mass meetings, paramilitary exercises, open contempt for parliamentary democracy, desire for autarky and for a stronger executive, concept of the corporate state and economy, and their anti-communism gave these movements their predominantly fascist appearance.

The internal political situation in France under the Popular Front government of 1936 contributed to the growth of fascism – the Prime Minister, Léon Blum, was a Jew, there were now eighty communist members of parliament instead of the previous twelve, and 2,000,000 workers occupying the factories to celebrate their political triumph. The property-owning bourgeoisie, fearing revolution, began to long for a strong man and to support fascist groups. In the summer of 1936, the former communist leader, Jacques Doriot, founded the *Parti Populaire Français* as a right-wing opposition movement. He who in 1934 had called in vain for a popular front, and had been expelled from his party for doing so, now formed a truly fascist party which was anti-communist, anti-capitalist and anti-democratic. It reached its peak in March 1937 when it had 137,000 members, two-thirds of whom were workers, but after that his party lost its influence until it received new impetus from the German occupation.

A far more dangerous element was the conspiratorial *Comité Secret d'Action Révolutionnaire* which was founded in 1936 by the marine engineer Eugène Deloncle as an underground movement. The purpose of this movement, which was organized on military lines, was to set up a dictatorship in order to prevent a communist revolution. It had considerable stores of arms and prepared to march on Paris, in the manner of its fascist exemplar; indeed, it was

Colonel de la Roque, leader of the French *Croix de Feu*.

clearly modelled on the examples of Italy and Nationalist Spain. Its *Cagoulards* (bandits) worked for the Italian secret police and did not shrink from political murders in the interests of fascist Italy, but it is doubtful whether Mussolini welcomed their support.

French fascism began to lose its influence once the Popular Front collapsed and Daladier set up his authoritarian system in 1938. Thus far it had merely been a kind of 'proto-fascism' and did not find its hour until the German occupation in 1940. Although the Vichy regime under Marshal Pétain, with its ideas of national revolution borrowed from the fascists and the French tradition before 1789, was not fascist in the proper sense, it did contain certain fascist elements, such as the anti-Semitic laws of October 1940 (though they were much milder than the Nuremberg Laws), the attempt to copy certain aspects of the Italian corporate state, the dissolution of the trade unions and the banning of strikes.

However, much of this remained mere window-dressing; even the first pre-condition of French fascism was lacking – partnership with Germany and Italy, which failed to come about because of their intransigence. Thus, the radical fascist groups, the *Rassemblement National Populaire* of the former socialist Marcel Déat, and Jacques Doriot's party, acquired influence only for a short time and then only as the henchmen of the Third Reich. As so often happens, the two leaders were in bitter conflict and united only for a short time in July 1941 when the *Légion des Volontaires Français contre le Bolchévisme* was founded. But even they were really only French patriots who in September 1943 unsuccessfully presented the Germans with a memorandum concerning the rebuilding of France. All that they could do was organize a militia to fight the French resistance and this only brutalized the internal political struggle. When they were both in exile in Germany after September 1944, Déat and Doriot fell out with each other for the last time; Doriot was killed in an air raid, and French fascism came to an end with the defeat of the Germans.

Fascism developed quite differently in Portugal, which had had an extreme right-wing movement of an ecclesiastical and nationalist kind since 1914. There were two groups who advocated a kind of social Catholicism combined with a literary nationalism, copied from the *Action Française* and Maurice Barrès. In this respect the Portuguese right wing was orientated totally towards France – this has been given the term 'Maurrasism' or 'gallicism'. Dr Antonio de Oliveira Salazar, who was later to become dictator of Portugal, belonged to this movement as a young student. They were called 'right-wing Jacobins' and these 'integralists' supported many attempted military putsches until the first republican dictatorship in Europe was set up in 1917–18 under General Sidonio Pais, a far more authoritarian ruler than Salazar was later. This was the first attempt to set up a corporate state, long before Mussolini and de Rivera, and was a completely independent development without any fascist predecessors.

The dictatorship of General Carmona, which began in May 1926, had little success in solving Portugal's pressing economic problems. Salazar was asked in 1928 to rejoin the government and undertake a budgetary reform; and in 1932 he accepted the post of Prime Minister. A 'guided democracy' was achieved, in the sense of an authoritarian, corporatist republic based on the moral values of the Catholic Church. In economic matters Salazar followed the example of Italy's 'Labour Charter', while the state militia and the state youth organization both clearly have 'fascistoid' tendencies. Nevertheless, even today Portugal is not a fascist state, but rather an elitist authoritarian state. One could perhaps call this regime 'clerico-fascist', although it is not so much the Church as a technocracy working according to Christian principles, that determines the future of the country.

Spain presents a similar problem: is 'Francoism' fascist or not? The sign of the 'Falange', Spain's fascist organization, can be seen painted on houses and church walls all over Spain, and until 1962 the

Marcel Déat, leader of the *Rassemblement National Populaire*, one of the largest French fascist movements of the 1930s. Personal animosity between Déat and Jacques Doriot, leader of the *Parti Populaire Français* prevented the unification of their respective parties. They acquired influence only for a short time and then only as the henchmen of the Third Reich.

Spanish radio played the Falange anthem before every broadcast. But it is the most committed Falangists who regard General Franco as a traitor to their cause. How has this situation come about?

The monarchist dictatorship of General Primo de Rivera from 1923 to 1930 was not fascist, although it contained more fascist elements than does General Franco's regime. Like the parties before it, it had no ideology and no doctrine its only aim was to put an end to the misgovernment (*desgobierno*) of Spain, in which it was quite successful until the world economic crisis came. It combatted Catalonian and Basque left-wing separatism, anarchy, wrong economic policies and the unsuccessful colonial policy in Morocco, but the system lacked the support of a mass movement and there was little real cooperation with the other fascist regimes in Europe. It did, however, have the following fascist characteristics: a charismatic leader, a controlled press, the army – and above all the officers' corps – as the main pillars of the state, a great state building programme, and cooperation between the dictator and leading socialists.

It was during this period of Primo de Rivera's dictatorship that the first fascist groups were formed, all following the Italian pattern. Another factor which should not be forgotten is that in 1933 leading Spanish intellectuals such as Ortega y Gasset and Miguel de Unamuno had expressed their disillusionment with the Spanish republic. Gil Robles, a politician who sought to imitate the system of Dollfuss in Austria, led a right-wing Christian party under the influence of militant Catholicism but it was not until 1934 that José Antonio Primo de Rivera, the son of the former dictator, founded the *Falange Española*, the Spanish Falange. It had anti-social and anti-liberal tendencies and stood for the united state against political parties. It wanted society to be structured on the lines of the old Estates, believing in power in Sorel's sense of the word as the most important political principle. It sought to win over the workers by promising to establish a totalitarian state without privileges of

any kind. When José Antonio Primo de Rivera was elected into parliament in 1933 he joined the other fascist groups in the *Falange Española de las Jons*.

The Falange was not able to achieve much political success before the generals intervened in 1936, and General Franco, when he became head of state, amalgamated the Falange with the Spanish monarchists to make a state unity party. His regime can not be termed fascist either, for it lacks many of the characteristics of true fascism. It is a conservative, authoritarian dictatorship largely run by Catholic technocrats.

In Great Britain fascist ideas originated in conservative hostility to the socialist workers' movement and to anti-imperialist liberalism. One need only refer to the books by Carthill: *A Lost Empire* (1923), and *The Legacy of Liberalism* (1924); the latter was published in German in the 1920s with an introduction by the Minister of Defence, Gessler. Other precursors were reformist politicians who were opposed to the unrestrained progress of technology, such as the Earl of Portsmouth (Viscount Lymington)

Above: General Franco and his victorious troops entering the besieged castle of Alcazar in Toledo in 1936.

Page 32: An armed column of young members of the *Falange Española*. It embraced the fascist anti-liberal ideology glorifying the state and worshipping its leader.

General Franco with Marshal Pétain, who headed the Vichy Government of unoccupied France, 1941–45. His regime was essentially fascist in character, though unlike Franco's, it had to toe the anti-semitic line under German pressure.

with his *Famine in England* and *Alternative to Death : the relationship between soil, family and community* (1943). There was also Lord Milner, 'the best civilian soldier in the British Empire', who said of himself that he was both left- and right-wing. Milner, an anti-parliamentarian, occupied several important posts in the Empire in the course of his political career. He thought only in terms of the state, rejecting the system of parliamentary parties. Educated in Germany, he planned to write a book about Ferdinand Lassalle and spoke contemptuously of the 'poisonous effect of the parties on national politics' and of the 'mob in Westminster'. He advocated social reform at home and protectionism throughout the Empire: a strong society and nation state were for him the basic pre-conditions of the British Empire. He rejected the League of Nations, advocating instead the cooperation of free nations. Major General J. F. C. Fuller expressed similar ideas a decade later. He had been Chief of General Staff of the Royal Tank Corps during the First World War and had become a distinguished military writer. In *The First of League Wars* his account of the war in Abyssinia in 1936 showed his positive attitude towards the Italians. He expressed his political views again in his *Memoirs of an Unconventional Soldier* (1937), which was also translated into German. For him the League of Nations and bolshevism were identical in their supranational aims. What he saw at that time was the struggle between a democracy which had outlived its purpose and fascism which was aspiring to power. He advocated a combination of scientific individualism and aristocracy, that is, the setting up of a corporative state – a development he thought inevitable in the machine age. What disturbed him about Italian fascism was the lack of personal freedom, for he believed that the ultimate aim of every state corporation could only be to develop the spirit of freedom, and in 1937 he was still convinced that the aim of fascism was to create a higher level of individual freedom.

Both Milner and Fuller saw the British Empire as a cooperation based on the principle of debate rather than on leadership from above: 'the strength of defence must be authoritative, the strength of production must be cooperative and the way of life must be individual.' Fuller acknowledged 'the proud army of dictators', Lenin, Stalin, Pilsudski, Kemal Atatürk, Mussolini, Hitler . . . In 1943 the Earl of Portsmouth feared that an alliance between Britain and the two most powerful industrial states in the world, the USA and USSR, might have disadvantages for Britain. He foresaw the emergence of the 'servile state'. In some respects his ideas were quite reactionary, such as when he spoke out against men working down in the mines instead of being healthily occupied in agricultural work, and he approved of the efforts made by the fascists to make agriculture a healthy and viable industry once more, though he was sceptical about their lasting effects. He appreciated the influence of the Catholic Church in bringing about a revitalization of agriculture in many countries. He was most indignant that his conservative ideas concerning the revitalization of British society should be denigrated by the catcalls against fascism and National Socialism, particularly as he rejected many aspects of fascism, such as its fanatical racialism.

Metropolitan State University
Library Services

It is not surprising, therefore, that fascism in Britain was in many respects very different from the continental varieties, if we look beyond the external appearances of uniforms, military parades and slogans. Although there were radical fascist movements in Britain after 1918, Sir Oswald Mosley was the real founder of British fascism. He was a former officer and was a conservative to begin with, but joined the Labour Party in 1924, and in 1929 became Chancellor of the Duchy of Lancaster in Ramsay Macdonald's second government at the age of thirty-three. He was given the special task of bringing unemployment to an end.

The peculiarly British quality of the movement was pronounced: Mosley disassociated himself from the continental varieties of fascism, though he knew the Italian and German leaders and respected them.

A mass rally of English fascists in Hyde Park with their leader, Oswald Mosley taking the salute. Often thousands of police were unable to quell the violent rioting that broke out between the fascists and their opponents.

He made this quite clear in his autobiography *My Life*, which was published in 1968. Interestingly, his reasons for this are ideological; he asserted that they had misunderstood Oswald Spengler's *Decline of the West*, whereas he had learned from Spengler that in times of national crisis a strong man, if he is supported by a mass movement, can halt the decline. Mosley's anti-Semitism was also less marked than that of the National Socialists. His British Union of Fascists had by 1936 adopted an openly anti-Semitic line, but it never emulated the extremism of the Germans. Significantly, Mosley was the only leader of a European fascist movement to have any clear economic theories.

He had no need of imperialist fantasies, for had his movement come to power he would have had the whole British Empire at his command. What he needed was a realistic programme of action to deal with the economic and social crisis affecting his country. He was a friend of John Maynard Keynes, who had convinced him of the necessity of his theory of 'productive spending'. Thus Mosley, both in the Labour Party and later in his short-lived New Party, advocated a state-planned economy, the storing of raw materials and foodstuffs, increased agricultural production and nationalization of the banks.

He might have remained a socialist for the rest of his life, like Mussolini, had he been able to satisfy himself that the socialist parties were really trying to put into practice what they constantly preached. But because his 'national programme' of 1930 could not be put into practice on account of the political atmosphere in Britain at that time, Mosley founded his New Party in March 1931. He was merely concerned with overcoming economic stagnation in Britain. His theories were based on pragmatism and were without any ideology. However, he lost the elections of October 1931 through the formation of the National Government.

Because Mosley was expelled from the Labour Party at the same time, he was, almost unconsciously, forced to the right; here too there is a parallel with Mussolini, but now Mosley became consciously

---

The TRUTH about Adolf Hitler's Battle for Civilisation!

How to Destroy the World's Destroyers!

HAIL HITLER!
HAIL JAPAN!
HAIL HENRY FORD!
The Three Outstanding Champions of Humanity.

Knock Out the Jews' Teeth; overthrow their Three Great Instruments of World Control
The Gold Standard,
The Soviet,
The League of Nations.

An excerpt from a pamphlet of the 'British fascists' portraying Hitler, Japan and Henry Ford as the great champions of humanity and demanding the overthrow of Jewish world control.

'fascistic'. His movement was provided with uniforms, like those of the Italian black-shirts, insignia, songs, and groups of strong-arm men to deal with left-wing opponents – a development similar to those in Germany and Italy. John Strachey, a leading ideologist in Mosley's party, but who soon left it, explained that at that time the party had had to choose between being identified either with the reactionary ruling class or with the workers who were in revolt.

Mosley chose the first, as Mussolini and Hitler had done at a certain point in their careers, and thus drew upon himself the enmity of the left. He organized his 'Biff Boys' and para-military groups to deal with this opposition – curiously, they were trained by the famous Jewish boxer, 'Kid' Lewis. Thus Mosley, following the example of Mussolini, allowed himself to be forced into a more radical, more militant, right-wing position. This culminated in October 1932 with the founding of the British Union of Fascists, which was from the beginning strongly anti-communist, after Mosley had visited Rome for the first time, in January, to study Italian fascism.

His great mistake was that, like the communists, he forecast the imminent collapse of the capitalist system. When this failed to happen he lost credibility; his influence on the British people began to dwindle and disappeared completely as the world economic crisis was gradually overcome, as the power of the government was increased through the National Government and as Britain turned against the Third Reich.

The development of fascism in Norway was very different. A land of three million inhabitants, situated in a remote corner of Europe, it had had a parliamentary democracy since 1814. However, early on a strong radical movement had developed among the workers in the flourishing shipping industry. In 1920 the first right-wing movements were formed to oppose it, in the form of ship owners' anti-strike organizations, as in Finland. In 1925 the anti-Marxist *Fredrelandslaag*, the Fatherland League,

was formed under the former Prime Minister, Christian Michelsen, and the famous polar explorer, Fridtjof Nansen. This nationalist, though not fascist, movement might have achieved considerable success in Norway had not both its leaders died prematurely, in 1925 and 1930. In 1931, Vidkun Quisling, a former general staff officer who had worked with Nansen for many years in Russian famine relief, founded the *Nordisk Folkereisning* which advocated an extreme Nordic racialism. He was a highly gifted, imaginative, but basically unpolitical man who, until he was killed in 1945, believed that Hitler had been his intellectual disciple.

After he was discharged from the army in 1923, his first ambition was to organize extreme left-wing 'Red Guards'. He then became Minister of War in the government of the Agrarian Party from 1931 to 1933. After its fall he founded the *Nasjonal Samling* in May 1933, which had considerable influential

Mosley became consciously fascistic. He provided his movement with uniforms like those of the Italian black-shirts, adopted their insignia and songs and employed groups of strong-arm men to deal with left-wing opponents. The theatrics at the meetings were similar to those of Hitler and Mussolini.

Vidkun Quisling, Premier and Foreign Minister of the Norwegian puppet government during World War II. He was the founder and leader of the tiny Norwegian Nazi organization — the *Nasjonal Samling* — and helped the Germans to prepare for and execute their invasion of Norway. He was shot as a collaborator in 1945.

support. His movement, which was anti-communist, anti-parliamentarian and racialist, made little headway in the years which followed, but its opportunity came in April 1940 with the German occupation. Yet Quisling remained no more than a German puppet, even when they made him Prime Minister in 1942. He never achieved his aim of signing a peace treaty with the Germans, any more than the rest of Hitler's puppets in occupied Europe did, and in the end his name became synonymous with traitor.

There was a similar development in Finland, although the country might easily have become fascist long before Hitler came to power. The hatred of the largely peasant population for the Russians who had ruled them until 1917, and for the Swedish upper classes, had early on developed into racialism. Like Norway, Finland also had a powerful extreme left-wing movement. As a result of Finland's loss of Karelia, Finnish irredentism and the call for a Greater Finland incorporating large tracts of the Soviet Union gained ground. The Finns saw themselves as guardians of European culture against the Asian barbarians. Behind them stood the military

Med Quisling for Norge

leaders of the battle for independence in 1918–19, Swinhufvud, and Generals Walden and Mannerheim. In 1920 Finland had an anti-parliamentary coalition party, an armed militia of volunteers and a completely fascist student organization which, long before Hitler and Mussolini, was advocating the same nationalist, imperialist, anti-democratic and anti-socialist programme; in the 1930s about eighty per cent of Finnish students belonged to it.

The effect of the world economic crisis on the Finnish timber industry, upon which the country depended, resulted in the formation of the stridently anti-communist peasant 'Lappo' movement, towards the end of 1929. This organization, which consisted of members of the ruling classes and large sections of the discontented peasants, wanted a strong government which would not shrink from force. They tended to copy the Italian fascists and it was partly on their advice that they marched on Helsinki in July 1930, but the movement also had certain National Socialist elements such as a marked anti-Semitism, although there were only a few hundred Jews in the whole of Finland. But after the

Lappo movement had begun to terrorize the government, and its attempted putsch in 1932 had been
suppressed, its political influence began to dwindle
until it disappeared altogether as a result of the Third
Reich's uncooperative attitude during the winter
campaign against the USSR in 1939–40. After that
there was no fascist party left in Finland to work with
the Germans in 1941.

The situation in the USSR was similar in effect
though different in structure. There were no fascist
or subversive organizations there in 1941. There
was, however, a Russian fascist movement amongst
the emigrants, who numbered 2,000,000 in 1917.
Like French *nationalisme intégral* it grew out of the
legitimist monarchist movement but never developed
into a mass movement, and like every opposition
movement dedicated to a return to the past, but not
rooted in its native soil, its areas of influence were
strictly limited. The younger generation in the USA
and Japan, dissatisfied with a monarchism which
was both obsolete and lacking in a political programme, formed fascist movements, but these too
had no clear programme and were always falling
out with each other. The 'All Russian Party', which
was founded in 1934, ended in ignominy in 1945
when its spiritual leader, Rodsayevsky, was executed
by Stalin, to whom he had surrendered. The same
fate befell General Vlasov, who had thought that he
could cooperate with the Germans.

Typological fascism

*Das Paradoxon des scheinbaren Noch-Bestehen-Könnens
bei tatsächlichem Ende.* (The illusion of continued
existence after death.)
                    HUGO VON HOFMANNSTHAL, 1928

Schwester, die Welt wird wieder gesund. (Sister, the world
will recover.)
                              IGNAZ SEIPEL, 1932

Having examined some of the fascist movements in
the first two European regions, let us now turn to
eastern central Europe, to Austria, Hungary, Poland
and Rumania. In all these countries the influence of
the Catholic Church is an important factor, so that
we can speak of 'clerico-fascism'. Austria is parti-

cularly interesting because it was the breeding-ground of National Socialism and the concept of the corporate state, and it was there that, according to Friedrich Heer, a form of 'fascistoid' state developed from 1932 to 1938, with close connections to fascist Italy and the Vatican. But this state was at conflict with itself and was only united in its opposition to National Socialist Germany. The conflict was between those who supported the concept of a German–Austrian corporate state with a Catholic, conservative bias, and those who supported the Italy-oriented *Heimwehr* led by Major Fey and Prince Starhemberg.

The process of building up a kind of corporate state under Chancellor Engelbert Dollfuss during the years 1932 to 1934 is generally called 'Austrofascism', as a particular form of clerical fascism. Others merely refer to Austria's 'authoritarian era' or to a 'bourgeois dictatorship'. Nolte considered Dollfuss's corporate state a mere 'defence metamorphosis'. Certainly Dollfuss, forced by his single-seat majority in parliament to adopt an increasingly authoritarian line, stood alone and under pressure from the Austrian National Socialists, the *Heimwehr*, the social democrats and Mussolini. Indeed, many of his slogans did sound like those of the National Socialists, such as 'Austria awake!', 'positive values', a 'healthy nation', the 'upholders of civilization', 'country folk', the 'awakened Austrian and his home-land' and the 'creation of employment'. We should also remember, however, that many of Hitler's ideas were taken from the earlier movement of Austrian National Socialism. Also, Dollfuss's political ideology was based on a long Austrian tradition, and if he had not been pressurized by his many opponents and even by his own confederates he would have gone his own way.

Dollfuss's philosophy had been rural, Catholic and conservative long before he became Chancellor. He did not have far to look to find his models – they were there in the corporative concepts of Vogelsang and Othmar Spann and in the living example of fascist Italy as well as in the Pope's social encyclicals;

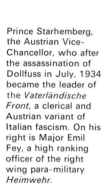

Prince Starhemberg, the Austrian Vice-Chancellor, who after the assassination of Dollfuss in July, 1934 became the leader of the *Vaterländische Front*, a clerical and Austrian variant of Italian fascism. On his right is Major Emil Fey, a high ranking officer of the right wing para-military *Heimwehr*.

'Austriam instaurare in Christo' (to restore Austria to Christ) was his aim, armed with the battle cry 'God wills it', and with a crusading ideology reminiscent of medieval times. He had been deeply affected, as the German Chancellor Brüning had been, by his war-time experiences and the spirit of comradeship at the front. Although he was interested in social reform, Dollfuss rejected the radical Austro–Marxist movement. He saw in the Austrian peasants 'the seeds of human rejuvenation'; he had a mystic belief in their strength and was so religious that he often believed he could feel the hand of God when he made political decisions. Although always leaning towards German nationalism, he was determined to engender a feeling of national identity among the Austrian masses, particularly after January 1933. Here he got dangerously close to clerical authoritarianism and *Heimwehr* fascism. For he, too, had an 'enabling law' passed on the basis of an Imperial law of 1917, and declared 1 May 1934 a national holiday to celebrate the 'conception of the new Austria'.

Although Dollfuss, because of his weak position in parliament, depended on the support of the Church, on the extremely influential Catholic student's union and on the Austrian peasants, he also had considerable support from the left, on account of his earlier work in the agricultural cooperative movement. But the left-wing radicalism of the republican *Schutzbund* and the right-wing radicalism of the *Heimwehr* gave him little room to manœuvre. Both wanted to force the outcome in a civil war, which then broke out on 12 February 1934. The brutal suppression of the socialists made Dollfuss's way towards the establishment of a clerical corporate state easier, but it also made him more dependent on the *Heimwehr*. Mussolini too was responsible for this development, for he had urged Dollfuss towards an anti-socialist position 'with just a touch of anti-Semitism', in order to use Austria as a kind of counter-weight to the Third Reich. His aim was to create a Rome–Vienna–Budapest axis and thus keep the Balkans out of the German sphere of influence. The 'Roman protocols' of March 1934 were to serve this purpose. Just as Mussolini preferred the German *Stahlhelm* to the more radical NSDAP and SA, so he supported Prince Starhemberg's *Heimwehr* in Austria with money and weapons. Again and again he urged Dollfuss to a *'coup d'état à la Heimwehr'*. When the Chancellor created the 'Patriotic Front' in March 1933 Mussolini was delighted, though his enthusiasm was for the elimination of parties and parliament, rather than for its medieval ideas. He wanted Austria to have 'internal reforms of a definitely fascist character' but Dollfuss did not want to follow in Italy's footsteps; he did not want to be fascist or dictatorial, he wanted his government to be Christian and authoritarian, based on a classless 'state patriotism'. But developments forced Dollfuss into a position where it was difficult to maintain the distinction between

The signing of the three-power agreement in Rome by Mussolini (left), Chancellor Dollfuss (leaning on desk), and the Hungarian Prime Minister Gömbös (far right). Mussolini, wanting to use Austria as a counter-balance to the Third Reich, was the architect of this Rome–Vienna–Budapest accord, which for a time, kept the Balkans out of the German sphere of influence.

authority and dictatorship; parties and parliament were dissolved and in their place a non-political, economic corporate assembly was set up. Instead of the despised 'formal' democracy there was now the strong leadership of a police state with the notorious *Anhalte-Lager* (internment camps) for political opponents, the socialists and National Socialists who made life difficult for the government by their acts of terrorism.

Dollfuss, whose position remained weak both at home and abroad, was forced to depend on the pro-fascist *Heimwehr* for support. This had been formed originally from the national defence organizations at the frontiers and in the big cities in 1918, and it had gained in political influence when the Christian Social Party began to use it was a para-military defence force. The movement came increasingly under Italian influence, although it was based on a strong feeling of Austrian nationalism, which was to be its ruin when the *Anschluss* (the union of Austria with Germany) took place in 1938. The riots in Vienna on 17 June 1927 and the burning of the Palace of Justice made the *Heimwehr* into the Christian Social government's strongest defence force besides the army. That day it was said 'signified the Cannae of Austrian freedom' (Heimito von Doderer). At that time the *Heimwehr* was about 150,000 strong.

It formulated its doctrine on 18 May 1930 with its *Korneuburger Eid* (Korneuburger Oath), according to which Austria was to be totally restructured and made into a people's state of national defence with the *Heimwehr* taking over state power. Its adherents stood for national unity and rejected western democracy with its parliamentary parties, the Marxist concept of the class struggle and the liberal economic system. Austria's new German national consciousness was to be founded on religious faith, the resolution of each individual and the leaders' commands. The leadership of the *Heimwehr* considered this programme thoroughly fascist. After Dollfuss was murdered in the National Socialist putsch on 25 July 1934, his successor, Kurt von Schuschnigg, began to suppress the political influence of the *Heimwehr* in order to prevent himself being pushed into a purely fascist position. This then deprived him of its force as a counter-balance to the Austrian and German National Socialists when Italian support failed to be forthcoming in 1938, as it had failed in 1934.

General Jozef Pilsudski's national and militaristic dictatorship in Poland had a very different character, in a country which was industrially under-developed, with an unstable political situation at home and a population two-thirds of which consisted of minorities. When the parliamentary system broke down Pilsudski marched on Warsaw with a few loyal cavalry regiments and took over power after a bloody battle. Politicians of such different persuasions as Count Carlo Sforza and August Thalheimer agreed in 1930 that Pilsudski's authoritarian regime was not a fascist dictatorship in the west European sense. As an old socialist he would never have got to power in 1926 without the support of the trade unions. Pilsudski was no demagogue and he even allowed a certain amount of opposition in parliament and in the press. He never formulated a doctrine; his main

Metropolitan State University
Library Services

purpose was to use his bureaucratic colonel's regime to bring some order and integrity into the Polish administration.

This limited 'militocracy' did become more authoritarian after the Marshal's death, but it never became completely fascist. It tried to organize a state party; it set up concentration camps to punish those who committed economic crimes and to intimidate the opposition, and created motorized party units which exacted taxes from the peasants in the south of the country. The extreme right wing of the National Party, which called itself the *Falanga*, formed the opposition; this group was extremely anti-Semitic and wanted Poland to have a foreign policy which was imperialist and militarist, although the state was not even capable of assimilating its large minority groups. Its ideology was greatly

Demonstrators in front of the burning Palace of Justice in Vienna, 1927, fired during an uprising by socialists discontented with the financial policies of the right-wing government. The revolt was speedily put down but gave rise to the foundation of the para-military *Heimwehr*.

influenced by fascist Italy; it was particularly attracted by the idea of a corporate economy. However much it may have admired Hitler, it remained extremely anti-German. There was no cooperation between the Polish fascists and the Germans after 1939.

It was different in Hungary where in the course of the war the hard-core fascists came to power. Economically, Hungary was as backward as Poland. A powerful irredentist movement existed among the people for, as a result of the peace treaties concluded in 1919, the country had shrunk from an area of 282,870 square kilometres down to 92,607, and its population from 18,000,000 to 7,900,000. In addition to this, the fact that in a predominantly agrarian country about half the land was owned by only 11,000 people created considerable social tension. The attempted land reforms only aggravated the situation, for they were insufficient; the new agrarian organizations were uneconomic, and there was altogether not enough intensive cultivation of the land.

Under the rule of Admiral Miklós Horthy, which lasted from the collapse of the Habsburg Monarchy and the brief interlude of the Socialist Republic under Béla Kun in 1919, until 1944, Hungary was a

Austrian National Socialists who had been interned in Yugoslavia after the abortive Nazi uprising in July 1934, on their way to Germany.

reactionary and authoritarian corporate state. It displayed philo-fascist tendencies only in its foreign policy, mainly when Gömbös was Prime Minister from 1932 to 1936. But Hungary was the first European country to have manifestly fascist groups in 1919 with racialist and terrorist tendencies, particularly in the officers' corps. During and after the suppression of Béla Kun's Republic these forces carried out a ruthless campaign of 'White terror' until a halt was called in 1921 by the government of Count Bethlen. They had even set up internment camps for their political opponents. These secret organizations became influential once more under Gömbös, until he too found it necessary to restrict their influence. Horthy's regime was supported mainly by the right-wing Christian National State Party, whose extremists were completely fascist. This group gained power towards the end of the war in 1943. The army, too, which had always had great influence, had extreme right-wing and imperialist ideas and practically ran its own government

Admiral Horthy, regent of Hungary, came to power in 1919 after defeating the short-lived Hungarian Communist Government under Béla Kun. He remained head of Hungary until the final stages of World War II, when the Germans, afraid he might conclude a separate peace with the U.S.S.R., replaced him with Szálasi, the leader of the Nazi-style Arrow Cross movement.

under Horthy. The radical fascists looked to Berlin for inspiration after 1936 – they dreamed of a Greater Hungary in the form of an agrarian, military state. The most influential of these was the 'Arrow Cross' party, an organization of former espionage officers in Szálasi's army. By the end of 1940 this movement, which, like the other two fascist groups, was openly supported by the Germans, had over 100,000 members. When Hungary was on the point of military collapse, the army and the fascist movements opposed Horthy and the ruling classes and supported the Germans. Hungary's existence as an

Ferenc Szálasi being told of his instatement as Prime Minister of Hungary. Backed by the German forces he replaced Admiral Horthy, who, as the victorious Russians approached, wanted to conclude a separate peace, and as leader of the Hungarian Nazi-type Arrow Cross movement, introduced a reign of terror.

independent state ended, as it had begun in 1919, in a 'White terror'.

Rumania is an even less suitable model for socio-logical analysis than the other eastern European countries which have been discussed. In the 1920s it was still almost totally agrarian. It had a very small middle class and proletariat – eighty per cent of the population consisted of peasants who were mostly poor. As a large section of the middle class consisted of Jewish merchants, Rumania had the oldest anti-Semitic movement in Europe. Educated young people, such as school and university students, although they were on their way to becoming middle class, still had their roots among the peasants who were largely ignored by the political parties. Also, the country was one of the few to benefit from the 1919 peace treaties, gaining large new areas of land. Thus it had no irredentist movement; instead it had the serious problem of integrating the new areas.

Cornelius Codreanu, the founder of Rumania's 'Iron Guard', an extremist, nationalist and anti-semitic movement.

As parliamentary democracy did not seem able to cope with all these problems, a radical fascist movement developed very early on in Moldavia, which had the highest proportion of Jews in the population and which bordered on communist Russia. This was the Iron Guard movement, led by Cornelius Zelia Codreanu. The movement did not have a definite ideological programme, its sole aim being to seize power and create a strong state. It would achieve this by means of superior discipline, readiness of action and the use of force, ranging from street fighting to political murder. It was a conspiratorial movement of great fanaticism and cohesion. Its legionaries who were organized into small units were ready to kill or be killed. They were also filled with religious zeal, and saw themselves as the hosts of the Archangel Michael. Not surprisingly the movement, which had won seventy seats in the elections of 1937, thus becoming the third most powerful party, soon came into conflict with government forces. In 1939 over a thousand legionaries were arrested with Codreanu and most of them were shot while attempting to escape. When General Antonescu became

General Antonescu with Horea Sima and leaders of the foreign mission at a parade of Iron Guard legionaries. The pro-German General Antonescu backed by the Rumanian Iron Guard under Horea Sima, assumed dictatorial power in Rumania and joined in the German attack on the U.S.S.R.

dictator of the country in 1940 he at first attempted to make use of the Iron Guard under Horea Sima, but suppressed it again after its attempted putsch in 1941.

Looking at these brief historical sketches of the fascist movements in eleven European countries, they seem to provide few bases for comparison, and thus would seem to preclude the development of a structural model which would account for them. The national variations would appear to be too great. Nevertheless, there are many elements which are common to almost all the movements, although sometimes they are only discernible on a regional basis. These include a strong religious element which developed into a crusading spirit; powerful anti-Semitic and anti-socialist feelings which often grew into a fanatical desire to destroy; and finally a fanatical nationalism and glorification of the army which in these countries was often enough the protector, if not supporter, of the fascist movements. But here too it is apparent that in none of these countries would any kind of fascist movement have come to power had it not been for the use made of them by the two big fascist powers, Germany and Italy, during the war.

Origins and precursors

The vast amount of literature on National Socialism that was published after 1945, in an attempt to make it somehow comprehensible, searched through German history for precursors, and managed to draw a line connecting Luther, Frederick II, Bismarck and Hitler. Of course there are certain ideas and actions which these personalities have in common with Hitler, but the differences between them, which are ignored here, are far greater. It is all too easy to look back over the centuries of Germany's political and intellectual history, to identify ideas or schools of thought that reveal a close affinity to one or other of the dominant strains in National Socialist ideology, and then to argue on the assumption *post hoc ergo propter hoc*. The quest for intellectual precursors always involves some degree of selective

Title page of Wilhelm Heinse's (1746–1803) *Ardinghello and the Isles of the Blessed.*

speculation or arbitrary choice, since this is in the nature of immaterial movements; but in the case of National Socialism this arbitrary factor becomes totally distorting. We have already suggested that Nazism, perhaps more than the other fascisms, was an essentially pragmatic hotchpotch of ideas, chosen almost at random and frequently wrenched out of their context. What is true of its programme is also true of its ideology. It is therefore inappropriate to think of Nazism as belonging to an intellectual school, in the sense of a strictly definable corpus of ideas with a history that can be traced from one representative to another. A catalogue of spiritual precursors, equivalent to the political line mentioned above, would be equally misleading unless the specific content of the 'borrowed' idea is made clear, together with the extent to which it is dissociated from its original context. Thus, although elements from the thought of early nineteenth-century thinkers such as Hegel, Herder, Fichte, Arndt and Jahn obviously have their place in the jumble of Nazi ideology, these are by no means proto-Nazis in the way that Saint-Simon can be described as a proto-Marxist. Not until we come to the already confused and second-hand racial and nationalist writings of the late nineteenth century can we begin to identify with any accuracy the figures that make up Nazism's intellectual background.

Similar attempts have been made to find the spiritual forbears of Italian and French fascism, and here the search is less hazardous. For France this begins with the desire to return to the pre-industrial, feudal era before the revolution of 1789. There were even links with some of the ideas of the Jacobins – even the most hard-line French fascists never rejected 'the ideas of 1789' as totally as the Germans did. After all, the Jacobins did discuss whether the will of the people was expressed directly by the people through an active minority, which is what they saw themselves as, or through the charisma of an individual. Jacobins and fascists had several elements in common – both groups were intolerant, both tended towards violence and were prepared to destroy their political opponents in the name of virtue or the Fatherland and both wanted, as a militant minority, to overcome the economic egoism of the bourgeoisie; finally, both formed cohesive fighting units.

The third development was the Caesarism and

Bonapartism of the two Napoleons. Napoleon III saw the nature of democracy as being crystallized in one individual personality and it is not surprising, therefore, that, when fascism began to appear, people soon began to compare it with 'Bonapartism'. The first to do so was the leader of the right-wing opposition group within the German communist party, August Thalheimer. In his search for the derivation of fascism he referred to Karl Marx's study, *The 18th Brumaire of Louis Napoleon* (1852), according to which the French bourgeoisie, following its power struggle with the working class in 1848–9, 'abandoned itself to a dictator and his band of henchmen'.

Thalheimer saw parallels between Bonapartism and fascism in that they both strengthened the economic and social position of the bourgeoisie, while weakening its political position; they both betrayed the interests of the working class while appearing to protect them from capitalism; both purported to be the permanent saviour of society, promising peace and security; and both found themselves in a dilemma created by their promises to economize on the one hand, and, on the other, to establish an enormously expanded administration necessary to accommodate all supporters.

Nevertheless, Thalheimer admitted that the differences were very great. For example, Bonapartism lacked the mass support that the fascist parties enjoyed. Napoleon's 'Society of 10 December' which consisted of many *déclassé* elements was only a poor substitute, so that he had to rely completely on the army.

In 1933 Count Sforza also found strong parallels between Bonapartism and Italian fascism – parliament rendered impotent, Prefects omnipotent, all regional or local government dismantled, any judge who refused obedience dismissed, and the universities and the press silenced. 'The deathly stillness of the nation is broken as often as possible by ceremonies, exhibitions, sporting events. . . .'

Tasca, on the other hand, whose subtle analysis in 1936 of 'Mussolinism' rejected any comparison of Italian fascism with historical predecessors, including Bonaparte, regarded such comparisons as pointless and as diverting attention from the real nature of fascism. Indeed, if we examine the common elements quoted by Thalheimer and Sforza we see that they could indeed be applied equally well to any authoritarian or dictatorial system of government. They are not typical of fascism, or if so only partially.

In France we come via the reactionary 'ultras', through Boulangism, Déroulède's League of Patriots and the *Camelots du Roi* of the national-conservative *Action Française* to the pure fascists such as Georges Valois.

When we examine European fascism we must not forget that its spiritual roots are conservative and reactionary as well as revolutionary. Things are further complicated by the fact that certain tendencies overlap. For instance, the conservative forces showed a marked anti-Semitism very early on, and the revolutionary forces did not. Also the conservatives, towards the end of the nineteenth century, were trying to develop from being elite parties into mass parties. Throughout the intellectual history of Europe we will come across thinkers who could be described in some way as precursors of fascist thought, even though there is nothing to link them directly with fascism in the twentieth century. The fascists themselves did not even lay claim to them. We discover the similarities only when examining their teachings. They include Niccolo Machiavelli, the Florentine historian and politician, Thomas Hobbes, with his theory of natural law and the war of all against all which must be overcome, and Giambattista Vico, the Neapolitan philosopher who saw world history as a spiral, rising and falling. We might also include Edmund Burke, a conservative writer who was a passionate critic of the French revolution, and the Scottish writer, Thomas Carlyle, in whose numerous historical works great individuals appear as driving forces in history. These are followed by the early socialists of the nineteenth century, such as Proudhon and Fourier, political writers such as Max Stirner and Houston

Georges Valois, leader of the French *Faisceau*, an early fascist group closely modelled on the Italian proto-type.

Stewart Chamberlain, the syndicalist Georges Sorel (1847–1922), and Vilfredo Pareto (1848–1923) and Gaetano Mosca (1858–1941). They could all be described as intellectual precursors of fascism, and they all directly inspired it, although no fascist leader, except Mussolini, would have been able to describe himself as their pupil. Most of them, and in particular the Germans, such as Hitler and Himmler, formed their ideas from secondary sources, and extremely dubious ones at that. Mussolini was one of the few of them who appears to have had a decent political and literary education.

The new middle class which was produced by the growth of industrialization at the beginning of the nineteenth century, stood between the educated and property-owning bourgeoisie and the rising working class. It lacked any firm intellectual position, it had no ideology. It was for this class that Stirner wrote *The Individual and His Own* in 1844. He wanted to help the individual, wedged helplessly between the capitalist and the working class, to regain a sense of his own personal power, the strength to live out his own egoism in the face of society. His disciples were individualists, anarchists and syndicalists.

Mussolini acknowledged an intellectual debt to Pareto; when he made him a senator, he described him as his greatest teacher because he had taken his teaching of the 'ruling class' and the circulation of new aristocracies very much to heart when he had first heard them from him as a young man in Lausanne. When Heller speaks of the 'neo-Machiavellianism of a disillusioned bourgeoisie', he links Machiavelli via Stirner and Pareto with Mussolini's fascism. When the German Chancellor Brüning visited him in 1930, Mussolini quoted several times the lines Goethe wrote as he stood in front of the great fountain at the Villa d'Este,

Uns hebt die Welle, verschlingt die Welle, und wir versinken.

(The wave lifts us, devours us, and we sink.)

This conservative, pessimistic view of life was closely related to the cyclical theories of Sorel, Pareto and

Ernst Jünger, distinguished right-wing writer whose militant nationalism helped to erode the credibility of the Weimar Republic, particularly among the young and politically uncommitted intellectuals.

Mosca, and brought Mussolini into direct line with the heroic realism of the Prussian nihilists, the new nationalists of the Weimar Republic, whose most distinguished representative was Ernst Jünger.

Pareto, as a disillusioned Mazzini-type liberal, formed his theory of the 'elites' as the decisive factor in history. Thus, like Mosca and Sorel, he helped to form a counter-ideology for the bourgeoisie to use against its socialist enemies. At the age of twenty-three Mosca had found the main part of his theory in the writings of Saint-Simon, according to whom there is an intermittent battle between the ruling class which wants to stay in power, and a new class which tries to take over that power. Mosca expressed this theory in 1896 in his *Elementi di scienza politica*; Pareto expressed his in 1916 in his *Trattato di sociologia generale*.

The difference between them was that Pareto used the graphical term 'elite', while Mosca spoke of the 'classe politica'. Both considered an ideology necessary as a means of support for the ruling elite, but neither credited it with having any moral value. Thus neither was of much use to fascism as a doctrine, for such regimes were based on the trusting faith of the masses. What must have appealed to the fascists was their idea, and that of Sorel, that the use of force was the determining factor in the circulation of elites.

In contrast to Pareto and Mosca, who both came from liberalism and remained under its influence, Georges Sorel, as a syndicalist, wanted to set the socialist workers' movement against the rising *Lumpenproletariat* which he had seen emerging during the era of Napoleon III. In this respect he was a revolutionary conservative, as Michael Freund described him in 1932. For a time he worked closely with the *Action Française* which revered him as 'notre maître Sorel'. He came to see the party as a 'false state'; all his hopes were pinned on direct action, the general strike of the organized workers. For him the proleteriat did not consist of the poor and downtrodden, but of the 'producers'. Every different socialism had a task to perform in its own country. Thus Sorel, like Pareto, welcomed Lenin's revolution in Russia, and Mussolini's march on Rome in 1922. To him the fascist producer and the bolshevik brigade-worker were his national- and class-conscious workers. If we read Ernst Jünger's study *Der Arbeiter, Herrschaft und Gestalt* written in 1932, we see how much Jünger is responsible for adding, with his 'Sorelianism', a new dimension to German thought. Thus intellectual links are forged between nations, as in all areas of political life.

While Sorel applied Bergson's *élan vital* to the proletariat, and attempted to infuse it with the myth of the general strike, he also supported the workers' involvement in wars of national liberation, for it was their country to defend. When Imperial Germany collapsed in 1918, Sorel called upon the German workers to take up the battle against the

Henri Bergson, whose philosophy of the life force (*élan vital*) exerted a certain influence on fascist thinking.

western democratic powers, in the spirit of Lassalle.

From 1910 to 1914 Sorel, disappointed with syndicalism, worked closely with the *Action Française*. Freund describes the meeting between Berth, a pupil of Sorel, and Georges Valois, a follower of Charles Maurras, as the moment when fascism was born. Similarly Maurice Barrès had allowed monarchists, republicans and socialists to write for his periodical *Cocarde*, as too Karl O. Paetel had done in his magazine, *Gegner*, during the last years of the Weimar Republic. Lenin, although he referred to Sorel as 'that notorious *Konfusionsrat*' (counsellor of confusion), was undoubtedly stimulated by him, and the same applies to Mussolini, who came across him through d'Annunzio.

Hitler's practical predecessors have already been mentioned. His intellectual origins were obviously Austrian–Bohemian Pan–Germanism and National Socialism. Mussolini had a practical predecessor too, in the eccentric shape of the poet Gabriele d'Annunzio, who, with his march on Fiume and establishment of a government there from September 1919 to January 1921, provided Mussolini with an intellectual as well as a practical basis on which to build up his fascist movement. D'Annunzio referred early on to the 'mangled victory', coined phrases such as 'A noi!' and 'Eia, Eia, alalà', which were later used by the fascists. His legionaries wore black shirts and carried daggers, they greeted their commander with shouts of 'Hail!' and their flags carried the death's head. D'Annunzio had already proclaimed the 'march on Rome' and his Expressionist poems had celebrated an imperialistic lust for conquest – 'Let us hoist our sails and set forth into the world!' He had spoken of the *quadriga imperiale*, which were desire, sensuality, pride and natural instinct. Maurice Barrès expressed similar ideas in 1894 in his collection of essays, *Du sang, de la volupté, de la mort*. Similar characteristics can be found in the poetry of Stefan George. In this respect fascism amongst the intellectuals developed out of the atmosphere of decadence and nihilism of the *fin de siècle* around 1900. The fascists also took over the fasces, the eagle

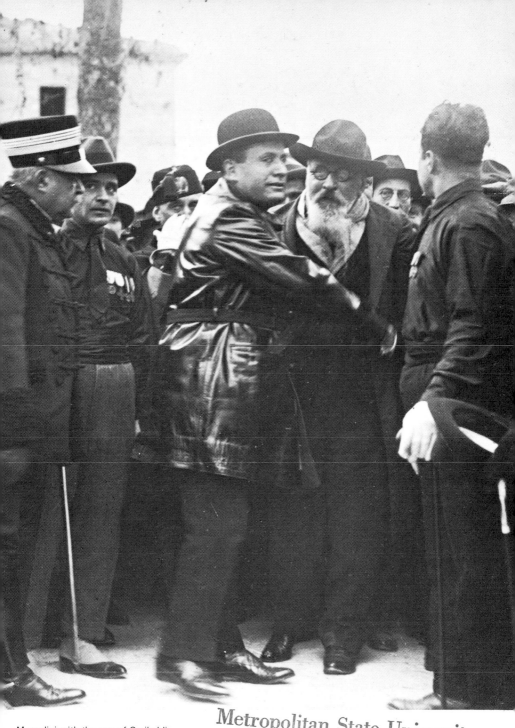

Mussolini with the son of Garibaldi.

Metropolitan State University
Library Services
St. Paul, MN 55106

and the truncheon from d'Annunzio. At this point Mussolini must have begun to fear lest he be overshadowed by the poet in his march to power. Everyone except the socialists was thinking of a march on Rome; the anarchist Malatesta, a former follower of Bakunin, had just returned from exile and wanted to make d'Annunzio's Fiume the base for an attack on Rome; certain Italian trade unions which had syndicalist tendencies, such as the seamen, wanted to join in; finally Mussolini published everything in his *Popolo d'Italia* and betrayed the whole undertaking. The way was now open for him.

Who were the actual precursors of fascism in Italy? Sforza relates how in the 1880s he read the works of the Neapolitan member of parliament, Rocco de Zerbi, who recommended a blood bath as a means of rejuvenating his country both morally and politically. According to Sforza, he must have been the first Italian nationalist. The first nationalist party leader was Enrico Corradini (1865–1931). He too was inspired by a decadent, Nietzschean *Weltanschauung*; purely aesthetically motivated, he advocated the elite, vehement action and the usurpation of power. He rejected the idea that the *Risorgimento* was a predecessor, as he did later, in the formulation of fascist doctrine. The only forbears he recognized were the Roman Empire, the era of the famous Italian city states during the Middle Ages and the Renaissance. His ideas were not nationalist but imperialistic, like those of the National Socialists later on. In December 1910 he founded the *Associazione Nationalista Italiana* which in February 1923 amalgamated with the *Partite Nazionale Fascista*. Corradini was made a senator, then a minister, and he brought several distinguished intellectuals in his party to fascism. Until 1932 they had great influence on the formation of fascist doctrine.

We must mention here the great intellectual influence of the literary movement, 'Imperialismo artistico', which flourished in Florence at the beginning of the century. There was also Italian futurism, which for a long time was involved with fascism. In 1909–10 Marinetti began to appear on

Opposite Mussolini in characteristic stance during the celebrations commemorating the foundation of Rome.

the public scene, with manifestoes and public meetings.

Although Mussolini and Corradini were in agreement over their veneration for the ancient Roman Empire and for the Catholic Church, as a Roman, political but not religious power, they differed in their attitude to the Risorgimento. In his periodical *Gerarchia* Mussolini declared that fascism would experience in European solidarity the wonderful Roman Catholic tradition which was founded on western universalism (*Convivenza mondiale*), and was related to Mazzini's concept of 'Terza Roma'. Hitler would never have proclaimed such agreement with European solidarity. Even though Mussolini, under the influence of Corradini's nationalist wing of the party, made several critical references to the Risorgimento, he never disowned it. The Risorgimento had given the nation unity and fascism would give it power.

Opposition groups (*fasci*) had first been formed in Italy in 1892–3. In Sicily the workers in the sulphur mines and on the large estates formed *fasci dei lavoratori*. They were also called *fasci rivoluzionari* and were brutally suppressed under the government of Crispi.

The Italian interventionists made use of this revolutionary concept of *fasci* after 1914 when, under the leadership of Mussolini and Filippo Corridoni, who was killed in the war, they formed *fasci di azione rivoluzionaria*. Their main idea was to get Italy to intervene on the side of the Entente. The first *fasci di azione rivoluzionaria* were formed in the beginning of 1915 and soon there were over 5,000 throughout Italy. In 1917 the defeat at Caporetto caused an increase in the numbers of those who wanted the war to be ended; so *fasci parlamentare* were formed, in an attempt to bolster the nation's will to defend itself.

When neither his front-line shock troops, the *arditi*, nor his attempt at parliamentary action seemed to work, Mussolini, on 23 March 1919, in a room in the Milan Chamber of Industry and Commerce, called for the formation of *fasci italiani di combattimento*. Those present, who numbered between two and three hundred, were ultra conservatives, anarcho-syndicalists, *arditi*, freemasons and futurists. Starting with fifty-one members, the movement had grown to between 2,000 and 3,000 by May 1920, with 118 *fasci*. Mussolini, the old socialist, was forced by his followers to agree to a tactic known as *fascismo agrario*. It meant the destruction of all that had been achieved by the socialist workers, mainly in the north Italian plain, by so-called punitive expeditions sent by the landowners and industrialists. The shock troops of the *squadri d'azione* and youths led by radical fascist leaders such as Balbo and Farinacci systematically destroyed all the houses of Italian socialists and communists and the buildings of the trade unions and consumer cooperatives. The work of decades was senselessly destroyed, while Mussolini looked on with horror; the memories of what he saw remained with him for the rest of his life, but if he was to satisfy his burning ambition he had to run with the wolves. He could only get to power with their help, and when he had done so they would largely dictate to him the laws of action. After he had come to power in 1922 the support of the monarchy, the army and the Church, as well as the land-owning bourgeoisie, made it possible for him to steer a middle way between the two power groups for a while, but the murder of the socialist MP Matteotti in June 1924 by radical fascists forced him into a right-wing radicalization rather than lose power completely, and led in a few years to fascist dictatorship which was total by the end of 1926.

Fascism was international and national at the same time. Was it therefore also a homogeneous European movement? At first Italy, like the Third Reich, rejected any idea of the 'export' of fascism to other countries. Here the question arises of the so-called 'fascist International', which even today is considered very important by the opponents of fascism. Immediately after he had seized power, Mussolini rejected any idea of 'exporting' his fascist doctrine – particularly as he did not yet have one. But by 1923

Metropolitan State University
Library Services

it was clear that he was weighing up the idea of founding a 'Black-shirt International'. But for the time being nothing happened.

Attempts had already been made in this direction; in Switzerland an 'international anti-Comintern Entente' had existed since 1921 to which various European fascist movements belonged. In Lausanne a *Centre international d'études sur le fascisme* was set up in 1927 under the directorship of Professor De Vries de Heckelingen. This philo-fascist institution published annual reports on international fascism. In December 1934 the International Fascist Congress was held at Montreux, but it had little international importance. Many representatives of fascist organizations, such as the Spanish Falange, did not take part. A similar attempt in Paris in 1937 failed in the same way because the leaders of European fascist movements which had come to power did not want to work together with the fascist movements in smaller countries, for fear of having their hands tied.

The insignia of the Italian *Partito Nazionale Fascista* with the *fasces*.

The introduction written by a well-known National Socialist, Edmund Marhefka, to an interesting collection of material compiled by Werner Haas, *Europa will leben, die nationalen Erneuerungsbewegungen in Wort und Bild* (Berlin, 1936) makes a point of some significance, namely that exclusiveness is an essential element of National Socialism. It aimed only at encompassing the members of its own race and people, in order to lead them to a racially pure, united society. National Socialism could not, therefore, be regarded as an 'exportable commodity' like communism.

However, this view that the two fascist powers had of themselves did not last long. The turning point came with the Spanish Civil War in 1936. As the fascists intensified their campaign against international socialism, Marxism and communism, their radicalism and their racialism grew. Now their attitude was that the world was coming to fascism, not the other way round.

Nevertheless, the concept of a 'fascist International' is a contradiction in itself. National differences alone were enough to prevent its being achieved. For the French radical right the enemy was Prussia, the Jews and Marxist socialism which they regarded as a German import. The French fascists accepted National Socialism as a *Weltanschauung*, but rejected the Third Reich as a political phenomenon. In his memoirs, Mosley points to the 1934 Austrian crisis which nearly provoked an outbreak of war between the two fascist regimes. 'It is true that these two leaders at a later stage came closer together; the antipathy of the Western World to both may have been a more potent influence than their mutual attraction.' The extreme nationalism of all the fascist movements made it impossible for them to put up a united front against communism or western democracy. Only during the war after 1940 was this effect achieved through the military strength and successes of the Germans, on whom the success and failure of international fascism depended.

The Walloon fascist leagues, such as the *Faisceau Belge*, the *Légion Nationale Belge*, and the *Action Nationale*, which were all anti-German, stood for the concept of a Greater Belgium, which would include Luxemburg and parts of the Netherlands. Their Flemish equivalent, the *Verbond van Dietsche Nationaalsolidaristen*, wanted to destroy Belgium and create a Great Netherlands together with

Insignia of the Flemish *Verbond van Dietsche Nationaalsolidaristen.*

French Flanders, which would then have a population of fifty million, and the colonial empire. These were opposed in their turn by the equivalent aims of the Dutch *Nationaal-Socialistische Beweging*, led by Adriaan Anton Mussert who also wanted to found a Greater Netherlands, but a Dutch rather than a Flemish one. During the war Mussert and Elias, the mayor of Ghent and leader of the *Vlaamsch National Verbond*, were bitter opponents. Himmler tried in vain to impose a German imperial viewpoint but all the west European fascists were afraid that this would ultimately make them the victims of German imperialism. If the Germans were victorious the best they could hope for would be to become governors of districts within the German empire,

The emblem of the Dutch *Nationaal–Socialistische Beweging* led by Adriaan Anton Mussert.

Holland's National
Socialist leader,
Mussert, at a party
rally of 16,000
supporters. In his
speech Mussert
boasted that the
number of his
supporters had risen
from 1,000 in 1932 to
40,000 in 1935.

and such reflected glory would hardly have made up
for their loss of political independence. In July 1943
Himmler explained to Mussert: 'If we are going to
establish the Greater German Reich we must have
strict discipline. Our main task is to introduce the
concept of the German Reich without having to
worry about everyday problems.' But in the Netherlands Mussert proclaimed in the press and at
meetings: everything for Great Germania (*Gross-
germania*), nothing for Great Germany (*Grossdeutschland*)! For the latter was nothing more than
German imperialism, and Hitler was like Napoleon.
No west European fascist leader was interested in
Great Germany. The fascists' extreme nationalism
led to strange and unrealistic judgements. Charles
Maurras went so far as to call the ideas of 1789 'a
German poison' which German thinkers had used
to sap the healthy French spirit, whereas in general
it is accepted that France had rid itself in 1789 of
the Germanic influence. In 1918 the nationalist

Léon Daudet declared that he did not in the slightest begrudge Germany the republic, democracy and socialism, for he wanted her to get the plague.

Polish fascism was decidedly anti-German, although it had taken over many of the ideological characteristics of National Socialism. In Hungarian fascism too there were anti-German elements, for example in the 'League of Turanian Hunters' which had several thousand members and was supported by the Horthy regime. It is interesting to observe how the two big fascist powers vied with each other in their attempts to influence the other fascist movements. Alfred Rosenberg did not consider Valois's *Faisceau des combattants et des producteurs* to be a fascist movement although Valois had built it up strictly according to the Italian model.

Long before 1936 the Italians began to regard fascism as an 'export article'. The fascist ideologist Rocco even thought in 1925 that the 'universal value of fascism' was that it was based on an organic and coherent doctrine, and that would be sufficient in itself to give a name and character to the twentieth

Fascist legionaries giving the salute, in Algeria.

century. Mussolini, who in 1930 had spoken out against the idea that fascism had a supra-national character, declared shortly afterwards that, as the spirit of fascism was universal in character, a fascist Europe was definitely foreseeable. After that Italian school books portrayed fascism as the 'creator of a new civilization'. After the September elections of 1930 in Germany, which resulted in the great National Socialist success, Mussolini declared: 'Whoever thinks that fascism is not an export article is wrong.' Vanity suppressed his earlier, better insight which had caused him to find the *Stahlhelm* in Germany and the *Heimwehr* in Austria more appealing. In 1932 the *Dottrina del Fascismo* stated that 'fascism now has the universality that all those doctrines have, which, as they are realized, represent another stage in the history of the human spirit.'

In August 1933 Mussolini welcomed the National Socialist revolution, declaring that now another great country had created 'the unitary, authoritarian, totalitarian, that is, fascist' state, which had destroyed the demo-social-liberal forces.

In general it is true to say that the two fascist powers preferred to work with authoritarian regimes and dictatorships. They only had recourse to purely fascist movements in the last resort. Mussolini preferred Brüning and Dollfuss to the German and Austrian National Socialists. Both powers worked with General Franco in Spain and not with the Falange; in France they preferred to work with Marshal Pétain after 1940, rather than with the fascists around Doriot and Déat. In Rumania Hitler supported General Antonescu and not the Iron Guard.

An examination of the history of the fascist movements in Europe from 1919 to 1945 shows that they were both national and international. It also shows that had not the fascists taken over power in Italy and Germany there would have been no fascism in Europe worth speaking of. In many cases a fascist movement had developed for purely nationalist, or even regional motives, such as the *Verbond van dietsche Nationaalsolidaristen* which was founded in October 1931 by Joris van Severen in order to protect the Flemish part of the Belgian population against domination by the francophile Walloons. In economic matters most of the fascist movements followed the example of Italy, even though they had borrowed many of their other ideas from the National Socialists. For example, the *Parti Socialiste National de France* was extremely anti-Semitic and against freemasonry, but in economics it stood for a 'corporative-syndicalist basis' and an 'integral corporativism' on the Italian model.

All the movements were strongly nationalist and thus hostile to the fascist movements in neighbouring countries and to national minorities. Thus, for example, the Iron Guard in Rumania was hostile to the Transylvanian Germans. If we compare the programmes of the European fascist movements we find there is a clear regional division between those which copied the Germans and those which copied the Italians. Generally the movements in the countries of the south and west of Europe tended to follow Italy, particularly those with populations of Romanic descent, whereas movements in the countries of the north and north west of Europe, where the populations were largely descended from Germanic tribes, followed the German National Socialists. This was taken as far as copying their programme word for word and their organization, like the Danish Nazi party led by Fritz Claussen, which had an SA (*Storm-Afdelinger*) with brown shirts, and an adapted Horst Wessel song. Also in Sweden the two fascist movements kept strictly to the German pattern, in their programme, the defence of their meeting-halls and youth groups. Their slogan was 'Sweden awake!' and they wore a yellow swastika on a blue background. In the Balkans the areas of influence overlapped. Hungary and Rumania had pro-German tendencies. Portugal copied France's *nationalisme intégral*, but was not actually fascist. The Austrian *Heimwehr* copied the Italians. Prince Starhemberg congratulated Mussolini on his victory in Abyssinia with the words 'long live the victory of fascism in the world!' Finland was an exception in so far as its right-wing

Fritz Claussen, leader of the Danish Nazi party.

extremists used Italian methods in their battle against communism and the socialists, destroying trade union buildings and left-wing printing presses. They wore black shirts and organized a march on Helsinki with the Italian ambassador as their advisor. The 'Swiss fascists' of Colonel Arthur Foujallaz and the British Union of Fascists also based themselves largely on the Italian model. They either had no anti-Semitism, or, if they had, it was of a more moderate kind.

The two fascist powers, Germany and Italy, were not only immensely important for all the fascist movements in Europe, but also for each other – they influenced each other's actions and ultimately each other's fates. In 1941 Hitler admitted that the march on Rome had been a turning point in history: 'The fact that they could do such a thing gave us inspiration.' Without this example, Hitler would probably not have attempted the putsch in November 1923; if Mussolini had been defeated, this would have discouraged him. Had the Munich putsch been successful, he would have followed it up with a march on Berlin. At that time he accepted Mussolini as his ideological and political model, and they seem to have had direct contact even before the putsch. In October 1923 Hitler wrote on the question of South Tyrol in the *Corriere Italiano*, acknowledging the Italian claims to strategic frontiers. On the other hand, Mussolini's sudden and violent conversion to imperialism in 1935–6 could not have taken place had it not been for the existence of the Third Reich. He was well aware of this, for he was very sensitive to suggestions that National Socialism, because of its superior strength, would eventually make fascist Italy dependent upon it. Mussolini showed his gratitude for the indirect support that Nazi Germany, merely by existing, had rendered his policy of expansion. After 1935–6 he showed a more positive attitude to his Big Brother, whereas before that he had been very critical towards Germany as a political power. As if unconsciously trying to outdo Hitler, he now took over many things which were not part

For the *Duce* on the 16th anniversary of the fascist militia.

Outsize canvas image of Mussolini at a camp, during the Abyssinian campaign.

of the tradition of the Italian people, such as the Prussian goose step as the *passo romano*, and the racial laws which in some cases were even more extreme than those of the Germans.

Despite the emphasis on the personal relationship between the two fascist leaders, we must never forget the motives of *Realpolitik* that lay behind it – each needed the other for protection against France. Despite Hitler's assumption of some of the external characteristics of fascism early on, and Mussolini's recourse to National Socialist methods later, any similarity between the two systems remained superficial. The two men, and the states they created, were fundamentally different. The famous friendship and the Axis pact came relatively late in the day as a result of the political situation.

The literature of the time reflects the long period of alienation between the two leaders which arose in particular over Austria. While *Der Grosse Brockhaus* (the standard German dictionary) of 1930 dealt with fascism objectively and in considerable detail, the supplementary volume published in 1935, which had to reflect the views of the National Socialist government, spoke of fundamental differences in attitude. For example, fascism was based on the state, and National Socialism on the *Volk*; then there was the rival claim to leadership made by the Latin-Mediterranean civilization in opposition to Germany's Nordic culture, and there was its rejection of any deviation from the Roman Catholic Church. The political alienation between fascism and National Socialism developed after the National Socialist putsch in Austria in 1934. After the 'Röhm putsch' which followed, Mussolini called Hitler a leader of murderers and pederasts.

In the above-mentioned survey of European fascist movements, Edmund Marhefka referred to the Third Reich and Italy in 1936 as the two gigantic pillars of European reconstruction. But in his view Italian fascism lacked the exclusive quality of National Socialism, having instead an 'expansive tendency' which pushed the racial question into the background. Thus from the point of view of foreign policy, fascism was less stable than National Socialism. To what extent these differences might have led to different policies, can only be a matter of conjecture. This diagnosis was totally wrong but at the time seemed to be true. The *Volksbrockhaus* in August 1937 gave short, objective and positive description, according to which Mussolini had founded the Fascist Party 'in order to promote unity, order, work, and the spirit of patriotism and to strengthen the state, from within and without'.

Basically National Socialism identified itself with fascism, although without accepting it as the general term. In 1935 Hitler wrote of fascism that it was 'the concept of the future state, as exemplified by its realization in Italy'. In the same way that Mussolini was a socialist and not a Marxist, he was also a National Socialist. But the difference remained. If jurists in Germany attempted in any way to subordinate the *Führerprinzip* (leadership principle) to that of the state, they were accused of 'fascism' by the party: the National Socialists believed that they had overcome the fascist principle of the 'impersonal state'.

In 1928 the nationalist Helmut Franke maintained

that it was actually a contradiction in terms to apply the concept of 'fascism' to Germany. That would only be justifiable if Germany took over the modern political methods of Italy. But this had been preceded by the Prussification of Italy, a process which, he believed, historians would later use to describe fascism. In Germany, however, fascist *Preussentum* would take over the conservative heritage.

The fundamental difference between Hitler and Mussolini was expressed by Hitler when he explained to Pirov, the South African Minister of Defence, that he was merely exporting an idea: this idea was not National Socialism, but anti-Semitism. Thus the Italian philosopher Del Noce came to the conclusion that the ideological alliance between Italy and the Third Reich was based on a misunderstanding – that of a non-existent agreement. There were, in his view, only two ways in which non-communists could confront communism. One was to challenge it, but that method would not overcome it. This was what Hitler had done. The other was the realization of socialism, which was what Mussolini had tried. When the partisans arrested Mussolini, their first question to him was 'Why did you betray us?' It was a question no one could have put to Hitler, for he had never been a socialist.

Perhaps the similarities and agreements between the two leading personalities were greater than those between the political systems they created. Of course, they came from different social backgrounds. Mussolini was of peasant origin, whereas Hitler came from the *petit bourgeoisie*. The former trained to become a teacher, and worked as one, although he did not like it. But Hitler lived as a social outcast, as a Bohemian. As a young man, Mussolini, under the influence of his life in Switzerland and his Russian friends such as Angelika Balabanova, had anarchist leanings and wrote for anarchist periodicals. Both left their country in order to avoid military service: Mussolini went to Switzerland and Hitler to Bavaria. However, in 1905–6 Mussolini did serve with the *Bersaglieri* in Verona. In the war both were good

Mussolini after his
arrest by the partisans
in April 1945.

soldiers, although neither was promoted. That is as
far as the parallels go. While Hitler lived in Munich
as a failed artist, Mussolini joined the Italian
Socialist Party, worked with Cesare Battista in
Trent and, a few years before the outbreak of war,
became the editor of the main socialist newspaper,
Avanti.

Even as a schoolboy Hitler had been a Pan-
German and an anti-Semite. The reading matter he
devoured so indiscriminately in Vienna served merely
to strengthen his preconceived notions. The same
happened during his imprisonment in Landsberg
in 1924. In contrast, Mussolini took his socialism
seriously, although in Trent it had begun to take
on a nationalist flavour. His early conflicts with the
leaders of the Socialist Party were caused by his
taking the revolutionary slogans too seriously, in
contrast to the Party leaders. But after 1910, while
editing his own socialist weekly, *La Lotta di Classe*,

he began to develop his ideas of fascism. Long before 1914 he was a nationalist irredentist, although still a socialist. At that time he regarded Austria-Hungary and Germany as Italy's main opponents in foreign affairs. Throughout his life his attitude towards Germany was a mixture of love and hate – he loved its literature but he feared its imperialism. By 1911 he had made a study of Reimer, an Austrian Pan-German who was an 'intellectual henchman of the Hohenzollerns'. He was already acquainted with their racial arrogance and their contempt for the alpine *Kurzschädel* (brachycephalic skull or cranium). He believed that the German people and their civilization (*Deutschtum*) had been poisoned over the last hundred years by the constant glorification of their own race. What brought about Mussolini's downfall was his vacillation between awareness of the danger to Italy posed by the superior strength of German fascism – even as a friend – and the temptation to let himself be carried along in the wake of Hitler's success, to share in his victories, for this was the only way he could see of being able to realize his own imperialist plans.

Just as Hitler, towards the end of the war, had remarked that he had been mistaken in treating the Italians as equal partners, so Mussolini, as the enforced leader of the Republic of Salò, traced the cause of the misery of the Italian people to the fact that Rome carried within its bosom four million slaves. Nevertheless he still raged against the ill treatment of Italian workers in Germany during the war, who were being 'torn to pieces by the Hun bloodhounds'. It was in Salò that he returned to his original intellectual position. He realized that the so-called 'New Order' in Europe was only a cover name for a German hegemony, the establishment of a protectorate in all countries. But the alternative that Mussolini had to offer could, in view of the world situation, only remain a wild fantasy – the introduction of world socialism, which in 1920 he had called 'infantile', and the restoration of the countries of Europe to their ethnic frontiers. He blamed the failure of fascism on the monarchy, which Hitler had called the 'aristocratic mafia', and on Badoglio. Their only concern, he maintained, had been to safeguard their class privileges. He had been forced by the fanatical fascists in the early days of the revolution to execute the men who after 1922 had tried to make fascism into a bourgeois national movement – Marshal de Bono and his son-in-law, the Minister of Foreign Affairs, Count Ciano. His life's aim, to prepare the Italian people for an imperial solution, had failed. He finally ended, like all the other fascist leaders in Europe, as a 'victim of German hegemony'.

Elements of fascism

Fascism is a phenomenon of enormous diversity, reflecting the differences in culture and historical background of each nation. This is illustrated by the variety of symbols used by different European fascist parties, in their uniforms, their flags and insignia, and also of course in their intellectual positions, as I have already discussed in the typology.

Nevertheless it is beyond doubt that different fascisms did have many aspects in common, both in their ideas and in practical politics. Ernst Nolte believed that this unity in the era of fascism was of greater significance than the sociological and national divergences. Fascism is not a result only of national history.

'Fascism' is – and this is generally agreed upon by the historians and sociologists – a thoroughly equivocal phenomenon. For instance, the war in Abyssinia is simply regarded as 'fascist aggression', as if monarchies and democracies had not waged colonial, imperialist wars of aggression. Individual characteristics of fascism can be identified in every other political system. It is the appearance of all the characteristics of the model 'fascism' simultaneously that makes a regime fascist.

We must also take into account how the fascisms saw themselves, though here great caution is needed. Again and again we come across the dual approach of the fascists who promised everything to everyone in order to get into power, and having done so pursued their own aims with ruthless determination. In 1922 Giovanni Zibordi, in his *Critica sozialista del fascismo*, pointed to the 'protean' nature of Italian fascism, but his remarks apply to all European fascisms. Before fascism came to power, he claimed, it had been a popular struggle in Fiume, while in the agrarian areas of north Italy it had been the hired instrument of the big land-owners used to force down the wages of the labourers; in Ferrara it had been for the workers; in Florence it had been supported mainly by students and intellectuals; in Romagna it was republican and in Rome it was monarchist. In this way it reflected the regional and social diversity of the Italian middle classes. According to Tasca, the importance of Mussolini for fascism, as it was in reality and not as he imagined it himself, lay in his dual ability to soothe the inflamed passions of the masses, and at the same time to allay the fears of the property-owning classes concerning their possessions. But here the differences are already apparent. In German National Socialism the radical tone of its ideology and its political aims was dominant right from the very beginning, but in Italian fascism this only began to develop as it grew closer to the Third Reich, and began to fall in line with National Socialism. Let us now examine in concrete terms the individual elements of fascism, as they emerged between 1918 and 1945.

An 'anti-movement'

The essential element of the fascist movements in Europe from 1918 to 1945 was their opposition to the prevailing tendencies of their era. This opposition was the most important part of their programme. They proudly declared themselves to be an 'anti-party', a 'counter-party'; for them a programme, a doctrine and an ideology were less important than their ruthless opposition to the enemies within and without, which Arturo Labriola referred to in 1925 as fascism's 'antination'. There was no political or economic power in Europe in the nineteenth and twentieth centuries that fascism would not have opposed. In its rejection of all the political and economic ideas which are often ascribed to the French Revolution, the 'ideas of 1789', fascism as the most powerful anti-movement was certainly a 'regressive phenomenon'. Salvatorelli described Italian fascism as the *Anti-Risorgimento*, and Curzio Malaparte

referred to fascism as a 'counter-Reformation'. An important Italian fascist periodical called itself *Anti-Europa.*

One of fascism's strongest motives was its opposition to any kind of internationalism, whether in the world of finance, in commerce or amongst the workers. What disturbed the fascists most of all about socialism was its international quality, and after that, the concept of the class struggle on a national level.

This extreme nationalist attitude on the part of the fascists, and their rejection of the ideas of the French Revolution, misled conservatives into think-

Above: Italian journalist, Curzio Malaparte, who first propagated and then opposed fascism, denouncing it as a counter-reformation.

Right: Masthead of an important Italian fascist periodical, *Antieuropa.*

ANTIEUROPA
NUOVEUROPA
RASSEGNA UNIVERSALE DEL FASCISMO

SOMMARIO
L'IDEA POLITICA

Asvero Gravelli: *Osservatorio:* Il vaticinio - « Gli italiani e gli stranieri devono sapere... » - Significato di un viaggio - Invito alla severità. — *: ITALO BALBO.* — ***: *Anti-britannica:* Uno che lo conosce - Strane meraviglie - Un altro che si confessa - Rettifica - Piccoli svaghi - Incorreggibili - A pronti contanti - Tiro a segno - Conti da saldare - Per finire. — A. Leonori-Cecina: *Constatazioni e anticipazioni:* Problemi della nuova Europa. — *Battute d'aspetto:* Quello della pelle - Quello del pugnale - Le loro intenzioni - Tutto un programma - La voce del cuore - Tre mesi dopo - Le due ombre.

ing that they were ideologically in agreement with them. It must have been pleasing to their ears to hear Mussolini proclaiming authority, discipline and hierarchy, instead of liberty, equality and fraternity as the proper scale of human values. This failure on the part of conservatives to appreciate the true nature of the National Socialist ideology was to have dire consequences for Germany.

This anti-attitude, expressed at its most extreme in the twenty-one point programme of Joseph Darnand's fascist militia in Vichy France from 1943 to 1944, was common to all the fascist movements. In 1924 the *Critica Fascista* said of fascism that it was quite clear in its negative programme, but was

Opposite: The 1936 Olympics, which in spite of vigorous liberal and left-wing protests throughout the world, were held in Berlin – capital of Hitler's Germany.

not at all clear about what it actually wanted to
achieve. Even the transition from fighting organization to political party, into which Mussolini, and
later Hitler, found themselves forced, shows that
they were quite prepared to take over tactics which
they condemned in their opponents. What they did
take seriously was their anti-individualism – expressed in the will of the *Führer* and of the people,
or in the total power of the state. Even here they
made something negative – the destruction of the
individual personality, respect for which is a
fundamental part of Christian thought in the west –
into something positive. Helmut Franke wrote in
1928: 'The idea behind German fascism . . . is
positive in its negation.' Nevertheless, fascism was
never able to deny that, with all its ideas and actions,
it developed out of liberalism and democracy, and
not from conservatism at all. In 1931 the National
Socialist historian Steding admitted that they
could not deny 'that we are the sons and heirs of
liberalism'. In 1932 Mussolini, in the *Dottrina
politica e sociale* of fascism, declared that fascism
could in fact be described as an 'organized, central-
ized and authoritarian democracy'. Many aspects in
Hitler's *Weltanschauung* and that of National Socialism can be seen to derive from the Pan-German ideas
and social Darwinism of the 1880s and 1890s.

Thus we see that fascism is by no means an
isolated phenomenon but that it is an integral part
of the history of political ideas in Europe. Where it
was entirely negative, as in the case of fascism among
the Russian émigrés, it had no potential for development. In the opinion of left-wing sociologists fascism
is always an immanent possibility within democracy
as long as this is controlled by society, but for conservative thinkers, on the other hand, it was this
radical democracy which had fascist traits. It became
clear early on that the elitist fascist party in Italy was
taking the place of the aristocracy which ruled in
the ancient democracies, only instead of an inherited
aristocracy there was now a meritocracy of the
Jacobin kind. Here too we see the Janus head of
fascism, on the one hand a mass party representing

a democratic mass movement, and yet at the same time the aristocratic minority of the fighting organizations (*arditi*, militia, *Freikorps* and SS) representing the anti-democratic elements of fascism. In 1928 M. J. Bonn pointed out that fascism, in spite of its violent character and its use of force, carried deep within it the 'characteristics of a liberation movement'. In his view the coercion of the minority by the majority, as is the practice in parliamentary democracies, was just as brutal as the coercion of the majority by the minority. In this, European fascism was anti-liberal, rather than anti-democratic. As Bonn pointed out, not only in General Primo de Rivera's Spain, but in other countries as well, fascism was basically not anti-democratic at all. What it wanted to achieve was a 'popular community of like-minded people'. In fascism, as in communism, the development was from a minority via the majority of a nation to a totality of community (*Volksgemeinschaft*). Thus General Ludendorff, who was by no means a National Socialist but merely an extreme nationalist, wrote in his study, *Der totale Krieg*, that the spiritual unity of the people provided the basis for total war. He traced the German defeat of 1918 back to the Jews and the Roman Church, via the intellectuals who had been 'stupefied by the occult and misled by the freemasons' and the 'working masses whose discontent was partly justified'. But how, according to Ludendorff, was this national unity to be achieved? He rejected all elements of the fascist or National Socialist ideology which could only be accepted by parts of the population. He wanted an absolutely united *Weltanschauung*.

General Ludendorff, who supported the Nazi leader's so-called 'beer cellar' putsch on 9 November, 1923, during which Hitler forced representatives of the Bavarian Government at gun-point to back a Mussolini-style 'march on Berlin' by his storm troopers.

Uomo sinistra sempre sinistra

A large part of the social programmes of the European fascist parties was taken up with social reform. But still it is constantly claimed that fascism acted as the protector of capitalism and aimed at suppressing the demands of the working class. In 1942, however, the American sociologist Talcott Parsons pointed out

The clash with socialism

that fascism was as deeply rooted in the social dynamics and the structure of society of its time as socialism had been in its early phase. Was socialism then in any form an element of fascism?

In his examination of the fascist opposition to communism, Del Noce distinguishes between the challenge posed by National Socialism and that posed by the development of Italian fascism. Mussolini was beyond all doubt a radical socialist as a result of his background; he remained one throughout his career and only his extreme nationalism prevented him from implementing it. In 1926 Margherita G. Sarfatti related how Lenin and Trotsky in 1919–20 had lamented the loss of Mussolini by Italian socialism; in their view he was the only one with enough energy to carry out the revolution. Mussolini's deviation from socialism was forced upon him by developments. The word gradually disappeared from his programme, to be replaced by the 'equitable distribution of capital'. Similarly the National Socialists replaced their original demand for the expropriation of property without compensation by a harmless phrase.

Other fascist movements in Europe, however, did take their socialism seriously, so the typology can include the term 'left-fascism'. The French fascists, Marcel Déat, Eugène Deloncle, Jacques Doriot, were all originally socialists who wanted to realize socialism in a national form. Mosley was also serious about the socialist elements in his fascism. He had developed his Keynesian economic theories in the Labour Party. His first concern was to put an end to unemployment and to establish a healthy economy, for Britain and the Empire did not share the problems of territory and population pressure claimed by continental nations. Drieu La Rochelle, several of whose friends later became leading communists, showed national bolshevik tendencies shortly before his death in early 1945. The Hungarian Arrow Cross party demanded radical land reform with the abolition of the big private estates. But Szálasi was not able to prove how seriously he meant his social revolutionary programme, for he came to power

A march-past of the
Francistes at the *Arc
de Triomphe* on
armistice day, 1934.

shortly before his country was defeated. It is in this
sense that Nolte refers to fascism's proximity to its
political opponent, because so many fascists had
earlier been socialists or syndicalists.

Whereas most of the leaders of the smaller fascist
movements, which would never have had any
influence but for the Second World War, basically
remained true to their socialist convictions, Mussolini
twice underwent a profound change in his political
beliefs. Before 1919 he, like Sorel, was in favour of
workers' uprisings, believing that they would have
the effect of infusing the workers with a sense of

A poster of the *Parti Socialiste National*. It reads: 'To die for the fatherland? Yes, always. To perish for the international Jewry? No, never.' The poster goes on to attack and denounce Jewish bankers, armament kings and corrupt parliamentarians.

tragic destiny. Time and time again he called for a revolutionary socialist minority which would create a new social order by force, and even when he became an interventionist after 1914 he wanted the war to have a socialist purpose. The documents which Matteotti published about the early stage of fascism show that the attitude of Mussolini and his comrades towards the workers was extremely positive. They fully supported the workers' demands. The first of the workers' actions, the occupation of factories, took place with the approval, and sometimes under the leadership, of the fascists. Mussolini wanted to educate the workers, to prepare them so that they would be able to run the factories themselves.

In the autumn of 1920 he realized that he could get to power with the help of the entrepreneurs, the *petit bourgeoisie* and the nationalists. So the cocardes disappeared from the fascist insignia and Mussolini stopped using the concept of class warfare in his speeches. But he was still trying to work with the socialists in 1922 when he was Prime Minister, and attempted to form a coalition with them. He spoke of his movement then as a form of 'fascist syndicalism'. Sorel had foreseen this – 'Believe me, Mussolini is no ordinary socialist' – and had suggested that one day they might see him at the head of a holy crusade, saluting the Italian flag with his sword. Mussolini was never a democrat in the sense of western parliamentary democracy. By the time the Italian army had suffered its heavy defeat in October 1917 he had realized the frailty of the liberal, democratic, parliamentary system, and had begun to advocate the idea of a socialist and nationalist revolution.

There was of course a wide divergence between Mussolini's own original idea of socialism and what happened under fascism. Italian fascism, together with other European fascist movements, such as those in Norway and Finland, started off and developed as an anti-strike movement. It can generally be said that although in theory the fascists were prepared to protect the interests of the poor and the unemployed, they did so only for as long as these coincided with the interests of the state.

These national fascist movements rejected the concept of class warfare, advocating instead a national community embracing all social classes. Thus fascism had an 'all-class' character. John Strachey, who was at one time Mosley's private secretary, and later his political opponent, spoke of the utopia of class reconciliation. In the classless society of fascism, the *égalité fasciste*, social conflicts would be eliminated or suppressed. It was not a question of one class being helped to victory, as in Marxism, but of all classes working together in the

Right: Flag bearers of the *Francistes*, a right-wing fascist organization, leaving Notre Dame Cathedral after a memorial service to commemorate comrades killed during the fascist riots of 6 February, 1934.

Above: Emblem of the French fascist organization, *Le Francisme.*

interests of the nation. But the fascist regimes were so dependent on the old ruling classes, with whose help they had come to power, that social compromise was achieved only at the workers' expense. In Italy during 1924–5 strikes were still permitted, but later the state clamped down on the workers. Neither in Italy nor in Germany did the workers' representatives in the political and economic organizations such as the National Socialist factory organization and the Italian ministry of corporations have any real influence.

In fascist regimes the concept of class warfare was transformed into the concept of warfare between nations. The battle was seen to be between the 'have-nots' and the land-owning, 'plutocratic' nations. This formed the basis of the aggressive, militaristic and imperialist element in fascism which will be discussed later. Among those responsible for this shift were Moeller van den Bruck in Germany and Enrico Corradini in Italy. Hitler went a step further and transferred this battle between the nations to the battle between the races, thus forming a basis for his anti-Semitism. As to his socialism, he was more interested in nationalizing the people than banks and factories, as he told Otto Strasser in 1930. Economic questions had little interest for him – what did interest him was racial breeding, *Menschenzüchtung*. But in the interests of armaments the economy was regulated on the strict lines of the war economy used in 1917–18. The 'real' socialists in the fascist regimes soon fell into disfavour or were eliminated. However, the establishment of a corporative economy in Italy in the 1920s showed that the planned economy was not unique to socialism. At the same time there was great interest in whether the experiment succeeded or failed.

Whatever the fascists' attitude towards socialism may have been, one thing is certain – they had nothing whatsoever to do with the left-wing parties after 1918. As early as 1928 an anonymous writer, 'Rerum italicarum scriptor', pointed out the inadequacy of the workers' parties, which had been weakened by a mass influx of disillusioned and disorganized radicals. Roused to revolutionary zeal by unemployment and the sharp rise in the cost of living, these radicals rejected all positive work, and demanded one strike after the other, aiming for a revolution on the Russian model; so for them, the worse conditions got, the better. In 1936 Tasca referred to the mistakes made by the Italian workers' parties, which had so lacked far-sighted and decisive leaders that they had under-estimated the danger of fascism, as the Germans had done before 1933. The socialists dismissed fascism as an internal concern of the bourgeoisie and they refused to defend the bourgeois government, although their own existence depended on it. The Italian communists fought fascism practically single-handed, but only after 1922, and by then it was too late.

Overleaf: Street fighting in Berlin in April 1919. Troops on their way to defend a Berlin suburb against armed and militant communist activists anxious to transform the 'democratic revolution' which had disposed of the Hohenzollern monarchy into a Bolshevik-style take-over by revolutionary militants.

Fascism only came to power after the left-wing 'revolution' had failed and the danger of bolshevism had passed. Even Mussolini admitted in July 1921 that there was no longer any danger of bolshevism. The fascists waited until their opponents had been weakened through government suppression and the awareness of their own failure before they followed up their advantage and set about destroying them. They would not have dared to stand up to a strong and self-confident opponent. Zibordi does not think that a Marxist revolution would have been possible in Italy because there was neither a powerful industrial bourgeoisie nor a large industrial proletariat.

The communist thesis that fascism arose as a result of the great crisis in capitalism and of the weakness of the workers' movement is therefore wrong. August Thalheimer observed in 1929 that fascism was not the ruling class's final act of desperation, but on the contrary, it was the 'expression of a growing strength within capitalist society, shown in a new form'. He suggested that whenever fascist movements came to power it was at a time when the working class was in a weak position – such as in France in 1850 and in Italy in 1922. But when he suggested in 1930 that Bonapartism and fascism represented the plain 'dictatorship of capital', this was an over-simplification. Nor was Bonn correct in 1928 when he suggested that fascism would have had little success but for the existence of the big industrialists. As we have seen, fascist regimes came to power in countries that had little industry, such as Finland and Rumania, and to some extent Italy. History shows that capitalist systems tend to support authoritarian governments, or even dictatorships, or strong presidential governments, as in Germany after 1930, but not fascist regimes which are seldom willing to share political power. Nor could the capitalists, as Turati pointed out in 1928, bear the idea of a fascist world entailing a permanent state of war and the division of the nation into a small select *Herrenrasse* (master race) represented by the party, and a vast race of slaves.

Fascism also had strongly anti-capitalist elements

in it which made it unsuitable as a partner for the capitalists. The ruling classes were aware of this, and thus when they allowed fascism to participate in government they tried to ensure that this was only in coalition governments which had various built-in safeguards. These attempts were unsuccessful owing to their under-estimation of the power-hungry nature of fascism.

The ideology of fascism

People tend to think of the programme, doctrine, ideology and *Weltanschauung* of fascism as motivating its political actions but, in fact, apart from the 'basic programme' of the NSDAP to which Hitler never felt bound anyway, it was the fascists' desire for action that made them cast around for an ideology. In 1919 Mussolini declared that 'our doctrine is action'. It was ten years before the Italian fascists managed to produce a doctrine, and then it was a hotchpotch made up of Mussolini's declarations, and excerpts from the philosophy of Gentile and the fascist historian Volpe.

Mirgeler speaks with justification of the 'basic agnosticism' of Italian fascism, and this applies equally well to National Socialism. In 1922 Zibordi in his *Critica sozialistica del fascismo* could find no sign of an ideology, although he paid tribute to the idealism of some of the fascist leaders. In 1919 when Mussolini had to fight his personal battle for political survival he had neither an ideology nor principles, a fact he freely admitted when he wrote an essay on fascist doctrine in 1932 in which he repeated the claim that the people did not look to him for ideology, but for improvements in their living conditions. From the very beginning he reiterated that fascism had no ready-made doctrine, but was designed to put into practice the doctrine of action. He had, like his opponents, regarded the fascist movement purely as an instrument for freeing the socialists from their 'drunken bolshevist frenzy' or as a weapon for the bourgeoisie to use to protect itself in the struggle with the proletariat. Mussolini proclaimed in April,

Metropolitan State University
Library Services

1919: 'We are realists intent upon solving practical problems.'

Wolfgang Schieder has rightly pointed out that we should not over-estimate fascism's 'apparent hostility to ideology', nor should we under-estimate its ideological 'fixations'. Neither Italian fascism nor National Socialism ever had a clearly defined doctrine. Both of them contained warring elements, for fascism never had a closed philosophical system like Marxism-Leninism. Mosley accepted Spengler's theory of a modern Caesarism and saw Bonapartism as its predecessor. Although Spengler himself had regarded fascism merely as a transition, a temporary solution, Mosley regarded him as the founder of fascist thought, proving once more the ambiguous and vague character of all fascist ideology. When Togliatti analysed Italian fascism in 1928, he admitted that it did have its own ideology, which he describes as the use of Marxist terminology in the service of bourgeois imperialism.

Although many fascist movements, like Codreanu's Iron Guard in Rumania, or authoritarian regimes like that of Marshal Pilsudski in Poland, had nothing to offer but a strong man who would establish law and order, they were undoubtedly 'ideological societies' – the ideology, or doctrine, the *Weltanschauung*, the *Volksidee*, in the sense of Sorel's 'myth', were all designed to give a moral and intellectual foundation to the faith of the masses in the rule of the elite. In Italy they had quickly learned that a bayonet was not enough, that it was also necessary to develop basic ideas. On the other hand Hitler, when he joined the *Deutsche Arbeiterpartei*, brought with him the elements of a *Weltanschauung* which he had worked out during his period in Vienna from 1908 to 1913. But this was based totally on negation, on hostility towards all the elements that had confronted him there – Jews, socialists, trade unions, parliament, democracy, the Austro-Hungarian monarchy and the masses crowded into the huge city. It took considerable time before he could develop a positive counterpart to all these negations. Both of these poles combined to form the 'fanatical *Weltanschauung*' which Hitler believed was essential to political action. Further proof of the importance of ideology in the fascist systems is given by the fact that, with the exception of fascist Italy and its idea of the corporate state, they showed little interest in economic matters. This is further evidence of the difference between the fascist and the National Socialist ideology. In analytical terms we can describe the Nazi system as the 'intensive German form' of fascism, and the Italian regime as a 'dictatorship for development'; in the former the important elements are *Volk* and race, and in the latter, the state and the economy.

Neither system could get away with not developing an ideology or a doctrine, but neither Hitler nor Mussolini had the slightest interest in proclaiming clearly formulated programmes as guide lines for political action. When Hitler announced his programme at the first mass meeting of the newly formed NSDAP on 24 February 1920, he was practically just reading it out. He did not feel at all involved in its formulation, nor did he ever pay much attention to it. What he wanted and intended was for his party comrades to believe in his power as a charismatic leader, and not in a programme which might tie his hands. Hitler's interest was not in ideas as such, but rather in their realization, and in the creation of an organization capable of active, practical political achievement. Tasca speaks in the same way of the ambivalent nature of Italian fascism. Had it been forced to justify its contradictions, it would soon have collapsed. The concepts which the fascisms used were purely normative and remained undefined, such as socialism, nation, worker, peasant, soldier, and many others. They were battle cries, conceptual signals, to make sure that the social revolution had taken place, at least in terms of language.

As with National Socialism, Mussolini's fascism came to power not on account of its programme but because of its strength in relation to the other movements. Its dynamism and its brutal activism won the support of the ruling circles, who thought they could make use of it for their own ends. Mussolini did not become a fascist as a result of having a fascist doctrine, but because Italian socialism was international and pacifist and, in his view, had betrayed the interests of the Italian people. It was not without a reason that so many syndicalists later became supporters of Mussolini.

Italian fascism originated in the *fasci d'azione rivoluzionaria* of 1914–15, and the *fasci di combattimento* of 1919. Mussolini had practically nothing to do with the formulation of their programmes. The *fasci* formed during the first years of the war wanted to force Italy into entering the war against the Central Powers. They had strongly anti-monarchist, republican and socialist tendencies, in that they saw the solving of the nationality problem as a pre-condition of political and social progress. Their ultimate aim was revolution and the building of a new society on the basis of a united nation.

The political demands of the *fasci di combattimento*, which were formulated at the meeting in Milan on 23 March 1919 when these were founded, differed considerably from Mussolini's views. They were far too left-wing for his taste, demanding universal franchise, abolition of the senate, the establishment of workers' councils in the factories, the introduction of a minimum wage, the eight-hour-day, workers' councils, participation in management, the transfer of management of both private and public concerns to responsible proletarian organizations, and old-age insurance from the age of fifty-five. A form of progressive taxation of capital would result in the part expropriation of privately owned capital, and in addition they demanded the confiscation of eighty-five per cent of all war profits as well as church funds. But just as Mosley would have found it impossible to put into practice Strachey's socialist programme of action because of the capitalists who were backing him financially, Mussolini too found that it was impossible, for by 1919 his *arditi* shock troops were being paid by big industry. Mussolini could not possibly advocate the extreme nationalist and socialist programme of the *fasci* central committee when he stood for election in Milan in 1919.

He lost this election, receiving only 5,000 out of 270,000 votes. He did make some radical demands, such as advocating a republic, a constitutional national assembly, universal franchise for both sexes, and abolition of the senate and the political police (the former anarchist showing himself); but the socialist content was far more cautiously phrased than in the March programme. In many ways it seemed to resemble the programme of President Woodrow Wilson who had visited Italy shortly before. Mussolini had welcomed him in Milan on behalf of the Union of Journalists. Thus in November he was demanding an end to secret diplomacy, the setting up of a European league of nations and recognition of basic political rights. The parallels with the Nazi programme of 1920 are astonishing – just as Mussolini borrowed many of Wilson's ideas, so the National Socialists borrowed from the Weimar Republic. In 1919 the new republic had done away with the Reich Settlement Act and tried to establish an economic parliament; the National Socialists demanded in their programme land reform and *Ständekammer* (Assembly of Estates).

After his election defeat in November 1919 Mussolini switched his emphasis to one of pragmatic action. For a time he lost all interest in programmes. In 1921 he declared that his movement had no fixed programme to be implemented by a certain date (Mussolini mentioned the year 2000), but sought day by day to realize those aims which were determined by the movement's will and passion. The government programme that Hitler presented at the Reichstag elections in February 1933 was similarly wide-ranging and superficially appealing. He advocated the restoration of the German people's spiritual and political unity, the protection of the family, national discipline, help for the peasants and farmers, elimination of unemployment, introduction of *Arbeitsdienst* (Labour Service) and settlement laws, medical and old age insurance, government retrenchment, elimination of the Versailles settlement, unification of the classes and protection of Christianity. Both Mussolini in 1919 and Hitler in 1933 made use of traditionalist and democratic sounding phrases to disguise their true intentions, and in order to win the support of the masses.

When Mussolini came to power in 1922 he was convinced, as Count Sforza suggests, 'with his hazy, encyclopaedic type of knowledge, such as any journalist has', that he would be able to solve all problems along the lines he had suggested in his leading articles. In 1933 important SA leaders said of Hitler: 'Our Adolf has still a lot to learn.' Later on, both he and Mussolini finished with the extremists who had taken the programme seriously. In the middle of 1921 the fascist *squadristi* forced their 'extermination' policy on to Mussolini. It was not until they murdered Matteotti, the socialist deputy, that he was forced to exclude them, but these elements gained control again in the Republic of Salò. Hitler brutally suppressed attempts made by his radical followers to instigate a second revolution; Mussolini was right when he commented later to Mosley: 'After the revolution there is always the question of the revolutionaries.' In the autumn of 1921 Mussolini referred to the suggestion that he return to his programme of 1919 as 'proof of infantilism or senility'.

When the fascists amalgamated with the nationalists under Corradini they gained a nationalist intellectual elite, which included Federzoni, Rocco and others. But their nationalist ideology was not enough. The nationalist *Tribuna* was merged with the fascist *Popolo d'Italia* in December 1925, thus integrating conservative and revolutionary nationalism within the fascist movement. But the resulting deification of the state could hardly serve as an ideology, and confirmed the intellectual sterility of fascism.

Giovanni Gentile (1875–1944), a philosopher and pupil of Benedetto Croce, attempted to fill this vacuum. On 21 April 1925 he published the 'Manifesto of the fascist intellectuals'. For the first time fascism made the claim to be an independent intellectual force. With the agreement of Mussolini, though against the views of many leading fascists,

Gentile established links between fascism and Mazzini and the *Risorgimento*. He portrayed fascism as the completion and not the destruction of democracy and syndicalist socialism.

His main opponent within the fascist elite was the former nationalist Alfredo Rocco, who was Mussolini's Minister of Justice for a time. Even before 1922 Rocco had spoken out on behalf of the amalgamation of fascism and nationalism, but also urged that the movement should free itself from its 'pseudo-revolutionary stigma'. Mussolini considered his speech in August 1925 on '*La dottrina politica del fascismo*' to have laid the foundations for the political theory of fascism. In practice, like Charles Maurras and Enrico Corradini, he was merely reiterating the nationalist theory of the enemy, the fundamental anti-position, the rejection of the Reformation, of European natural law evolved in the seventeenth and eighteenth centuries, the revolutions in England, the United States and France, liberalism, democracy and socialism. In his view the sacrifice of the individual in the service of the state could be the only justification of war, which would otherwise be a 'monstrous idiocy'. Ultimately fascism was for him action and feeling.

Thus Rocco was the real ideologist of Italian fascism, while Gentile was tolerated for export purposes. But faced with the world economic crisis, Rocco's idea proved inadequate. By 1932 the fascist doctrine was a conglomerate of the ideas of Mussolini, Gentile and Volpe.

In addition to this official doctrine there was also an ideology for popular consumption – a kind of universalist and imperialist neo-paganism borrowed from imperial Roman ideas. After his defeat in the elections of 1919 Mussolini expressed his contempt for all the versions of Christianity, and for all faiths, ranging from the Christian to the Marxist. Ultimately he was anti-Christian, like all his intellectual and spiritual teachers, but in favour of the Roman Catholic Church, with the emphasis on the 'Roman'.

The literary work of Baron Julius Evola, who published his most important work, *Imperialismo*

Pagano, in 1928, was characteristic of this radical, spiritual movement within fascism. In practice he was isolated in fascist Italy, being the only one there to advocate Nordic, Aryan and anti-Semitic ideas. Like all fascists he rejected all the forms of government evolved during the nineteenth and twentieth centuries, advocating instead the strict discipline of the elite. He was an extreme anti-Semite, in opposition to the official fascist doctrine, and totally rejected the socialist elements in fascism, believing them to be 'bolshevist'. He was a fascist only in a strictly limited sense, for in 1928 he was still hoping for the return of a new kind of Middle Ages and for the arrival of a sacred ruler. He had strong reservations against left-wing fascism. He welcomed the 'Harzburg Front' in Germany as a movement uniting fascism and conservatism, while his anti-socialist and restorational ideas led him to favour an alliance between Italy, Germany and Austria. Although Evola had little political influence, the significance of his extreme ideology should not be under-estimated.

A decisive factor for fascists of all shades was not the programme nor any artificially created doctrine, but the modern philosophy of activism, of violence. An Italian air force officer, de Pinedo, wrote in 1928: 'A dagger between our teeth, bombs in our hands and in our hearts an utter contempt for danger.' A letter written by a young German air force officer from Poland in September 1939 during the invasion is in similar vein, expressing the belief that the 'order' created in Poland would endure 'or else Europe, including England, will be reduced to ashes'. They would deal with recalcitrant Poles and others 'with a totally new, German discipline'. According to the cyclical theories of Vico, Nietzsche, Pareto, Spengler and other philosophers, every nation undergoes at some point a new consciousness, a kind of spiritual mutation, apparently unconnected with its previous history. According to Del Noce, it is at this moment that the meaning of history is revealed. Therefore the absolute defeat of fascism led to its total disappearance as a significant power.

However much the European fascists inveighed against historicism, denouncing it as a decadent phenomenon, the fact remains that they were also dependent upon it. They took all their arguments from history, thus proving that fascism was itself only an aspect of European historicism. Fascism arose in conditions of social disintegration; in the midst of revolutionary upheaval, people were looking for some new kind of stability. Mirgeler discovered that the fascists were looking for new models and rules, but searching for them in a world that, with all its values and traditions, had long since vanished. This was the reactionary side of fascism that tried to use history to disguise its revolutionary side.

But you, Roman, must remember that you have to guide the nations by your authority, for this is to be your skill, to graft tradition onto peace, to show mercy to the conquered, and to wage war until the haughty are brought low.

VIRGIL, *The Aeneid* (Penguin Classics ed.)

What was then the state of National Socialism, the German form of fascism? In 1942 Himmler, the SS leader and Chief of the German police, complained that for too long the Germans had forgotten 'that we are *Germanen*'. The concept of the National Socialist Reich, based on this idea, underwent considerable changes in the course of the years. At the beginning, from 1918 to 1933 and even until 1938, it was the concept of a German *völkisch* state that would overcome Versailles and the shameful rule of the Weimar Republic. Geo-political arguments of the Haushofer school of thought played an important role, for they explained Hitler's voluntary renunciation of his claims to South Tyrol, for geographico-strategic reasons. Hitler never thought along *völkisch* lines – his aims were always national and imperialistic.

From 1938 to 1940, Hitler built up his *Grossdeutschland*. It had been his idea from the very beginning; he was obsessed with the desire for a powerful Germany. The *Reichsidee*, the concept of a new German nationalism after 1918, was alien to him, but was taken up by the SS during the war. Goebbels expressed this new concept in April 1940 – National Socialism was going to carry out in other countries the revolution that it had already experienced in its own country. The main slogan was *Lebensraum*, which everybody could interpret as he wanted. Hitler and his henchmen regarded the idea of a unification of Europe by means of a peacefully negotiated international agreement 'as an impossible, childish fantasy'. Unification could only be achieved through a battle for hegemony among nations of equal stature. The *Kleinstaatengerümpel* (the jumble of little states) of Europe must be liquidated as quickly as possible, and long before 1933 Hitler had dreamed of founding a 'holy Germanic Empire of the German people'. The *Grossdeutsches Reich* of 1938–40 was followed by the concept of the *Germanisches Reich* and then after 1941 by the *Germanisch-Gotisches Reich* which would stretch as far as the Urals. Finally, after the military victories had ceased, he dreamed of a Gothic-Fran- conian-Carolingian Empire. Himmler thought that Germany was entitled to this although the other nations were not yet aware of the fact.

There had been time enough before the war for the Germans to learn something about the relation- ship of the Reich to its neighbours. But from the very beginning they were trapped by clichés. In 1938 Walter Frank, in his introduction to *Das Reich und die Krankheit der europäischen Kultur*, the history of the new Germany written by Steding for his *Reich- sinstitut*, asked the puzzled question: 'Why are almost all the Germanic peoples against us?' Steding referred to the neutral states, like Belgium, the Netherlands and Scandinavia, as 'a landscape with no history'. Like Hamsun, he inveighed against the *Verschweizerung* (Swissification) of these peoples, their hostility to the Reich, their disunity, their self- doubts, their lack of Great Power ambition, and all that he described as Europe's sickness.

Apart from the slogan about 'common German feeling', Steding had nothing to offer. Frankfurt and the Hanseatic towns were for him like Basle

Opposite: Heinrich Himmler, head of the Gestapo and the dreaded black-shirted SS. He was one of Hitler's most faithful lieutenants and, implicitly believing in his leader's racialist views, organized the extermination of six million Jews.

Sven Hedin, a well-known Swedish explorer and philosopher with Hitler, whom he greatly admired.

and Zürich, the breeding grounds for 'Asiatic germs' which were the cause of the German sickness. In his view, one farm on the Lüneburg Heath did more to help create the Reich than the endless rows of houses in the Hanseatic towns. He did not consider Austria to be ready for the *Anschluss* – individuals would have to be destroyed and at best a whole generation would have to be broken spiritually. He pointed out that the German-Italian axis was indicative of the way in which the foreign policy of the Third Reich went beyond the bounds of 'common German feeling'. He lamented the 'totally incomprehensible, unfounded and nationally undignified veneration of fascist Italy'.

This helps to explain the positive attitude of the SS towards Steding's work. Himmler's Christmas message in 1935 – 'More ancient and more eternal than Rome is this our Germany' – was the German antithesis to Mussolini's effusions. He too saw German history as determined almost exclusively by the peasants. His 'Germanic' ideology was politically unreal. He wanted to incorporate the 'Germanic' countries, Flanders, the Walloon lands, Denmark and Norway. He and Hitler both regretted that Sweden – the Swedes being the purest Germanic race in Europe, according to Sven Hedin – could not be included. Switzerland was an 'effete branch of our people'; like Iceland it should be developed into an armed bastion of Europe. In the centre a Lotharingian Empire would stretch as far as the Mediterranean, as it had in the early Middle Ages.

But as the Europeans of other countries, including fascists, rejected the idea of German hegemony, and the Russian counter-attack grew more determined, the Germans realized that the *grossdeutsch* concept alone was not enough, so they adopted Charlemagne, the *Sachsenschlächter* (scourge of the Saxons), to be Hitler's precursor as founder of the Reich. They then tried to unite Europe in an anti-bolshevik crusade. The SS spoke of the future of the west, and of the sense of western common destiny. But this concept was separated from all historical values that the National Socialists did not care for, such as Christianity, democracy and so on. The blood relationship that had developed between the peoples of Europe as a result of the migrations was to be broken up. They no longer spoke of the *Grossgermanisches Reich* but referred to the 'New Order' and the 'New Europe', without going into any concrete details that might have reassured the small nations about their future.

This desire to expand eastwards had its origins in the fear of suffocating in Europe, as experienced in the blockades of the First World War, and proclaimed in the geopolitical teachings of Albrecht and Karl Haushofer.

With the aid of the Germanic western and northern European peoples, they wanted to carry out the 'ruthless Germanization' of the Poles and the Russians in eastern Europe. According to the *Generalplan Ost* of the SS in 1941, out of forty-one million aliens in eastern Europe, thirty-one million were to be evacuated, and the remaining fourteen were to be *eingedeutscht* (Germanized). Fortified villages with bell-towers were to be the symbols and guarantors of this Germanization. The ideology was to become a brutal and bloody reality.

Major General Karl Haushofer whose geopolitical teachings powerfully influenced Hitler. **Below**: His son, the poet and dramatist, Albrecht Haushofer, who worked with his father and was a consultant to the German foreign ministry. Increasing disillusionment with the barbaric realities of Nazi power drove him to oppose the Hitler regime and work for its overthrow.

The great misunderstanding

There were few fascists who were really conservative in their thinking, although many conservatives had fascist sympathies. The misunderstanding lay mainly on the conservative side, where they tended to leap to the conclusion that the agreement in their use of concepts also guaranteed an agreement when it came to political action. The measure of agreement over concepts was indeed considerable. In March 1919 Mussolini had declared that fascism was in fact conservative, for there was much to be conserved in western civilization.

Conservative ideology contained many elements that were later taken up again by the fascists. But the rigid concept of class and the basically anti-democratic attitudes made the agreement a merely superficial one. This misunderstanding was further increased by the fact that the conservative parties, which had until then been exclusive to the nobility and gentry, were by the turn of the century beginning to develop into modern mass parties, giving up their refined manners and making increasing use of dema-gogic methods. So in the twentieth century several European states ended up with fascist regimes be-cause the conservative forces thought they could use fascism to tame the masses. They were successful only in Finland because there the conservatives used the fascist Lappo movement to get to power, which in turn led them to attempt a putsch which proved fatal to the movement. And in Germany the events of 30 June 1934 put an end to the endeavours of the nationalist right wing. In Italy it was presented with one more chance as Mussolini began to lose the war.

What Nolte calls the 'non-identical identity' of fascism with the bourgeoisie can be applied to the relationship of fascism to the conservative circles. There were many points of agreement between the two political movements, but their underlying assumptions were different and they came to funda-mentally different conclusions. The conservatives' preference for authoritarian monarchy led to their sometimes being described as 'potential forerunners' of fascism. The Italian fascists' *scala delle Gerarchie* and the elitist thought behind the Nazi order were both similar to extreme conservative ideas. Another characteristic common to both movements was a deep pessimism which was combined with a certain amount of contempt for human nature and a historical attitude that believed in the cyclical theory and rejected the optimistic belief in progress. However, the conservative looks backward in every way, ideologically as well as practically, whereas the fascist looks backwards only partly – according to Adorno he is a pseudo-revolutionary, a rebel. Thus the convinced conservative sees fascism as the result of democracy. In its attempt to revert, ideologically, to pre-capitalist, pre-industrial and pre-revolutionary feudalism, it in fact encourages the development of national societies. Mosley maintained that fascism would not have brought about any violent cultural break 'because in essence it preserved and restored classic European values'.

For the fascists history was a temptation to anachronism, as Mirgeler has pointed out. It was a temptation for them to go back in time. They rejected all the modern developments that had taken place in Europe since 1789. The fear that modern men have of constantly changing social conditions and of decadence led them to be attracted to fascism, which sought to overcome these psychological inhibitions by returning to nature – although to a nature where, according to social Darwinism, strife prevailed and only the fittest survived. This attempt to construct an archaic philosophy will be discussed later in the typology of the fascist image of humanity. A number of problems still remain to be discussed, such as 'the simultaneity of everything that has been and which no longer exists', as Karl Kraus formulated it in 1933. Mussolini and Hitler wanted to return to a time long before 1789, to pre-Christian times. This desire to return to pre-Christian times was common to almost all the European fascists. The National Socialists revered the *Germanen* (ancient Germanic tribes) and the French fascists the Celts, and the Finns the mythical, *völkisch* divinity (common to them, the Estonians and the

Hungarians) in whose name they claimed territories stretching as far as the Urals. Thus, by attempting to return to *völkisch* times, to the irrationality of early human history, the European fascists withdrew from the realm of politics, and gave up the attempt to conquer the world by rational means. In 1928 Turati recognized this tendency on the part of fascism to turn back to archaic ways of life. In French fascism too there were strong tendencies to return to the era before 1789.

Revolutionaries as reactionaries

From the ideological point of view fascism was a completely reactionary, backward-looking *Weltanschauung* of the lower middle classes sandwiched between the powerful organizations of the upper bourgeoisie and of the working class. They used their ideology of the return to pastoral life to counteract the ideology of the rationalization of society. In practice it turned out differently, and they only succeeded in furthering these developments. According to G. A. Borgese in 1938 the fascists thus made use of the methods of the left-wing revolutionaries and the techniques of the machine age to bring about a revolutionary upheaval. Fascism was a strange mixture of revolution and reaction. This was illustrated very clearly by Mussolini when he turned interventionist, thus resembling that '*ci-devant* Communard, who poured holy water in his petrol', as Romain Rolland said to Charles Péguy.

Nevertheless, as Seton-Watson points out, the fascist movements were still anti-reactionary, revolutionary mass movements. If the fascist regimes were to realize their nationalistic and imperialist aims, they would have to disregard the reactionary traditions in their own programme and those of their allies, and build up a modern, progressive industrial society. The real conservatives realized this early on: because no society can develop backwards, society could not go back to being conservative; hence a certain affinity between liberalism and its heirs (cf. Carthill's *The Legacy of Liberalism*) and its successor, fascism. In 1930 Count Sforza wrote of early fascism that 'many had hoped that it would be beneficial to the nation', for it was not without 'a certain fiery idealism'. After 30 January 1933 the last of the German liberals voted for Hitler until they were forced to disband. Fascism would not have won such a hold on the bourgeoisie so quickly but for the support of the big Italian newspapers. The liberal philosopher Giovanni Gentile went over to the fascists with the minority of the Italian liberals. The pluralistic-parliamentarian system of liberalism, so similar to that of the ancient 'democracy', is not basically different from the structure of totalitarian regimes.

One can even go so far as to say that fascism, by wanting to give the class struggle and modern mass society national aims, was in fact related to those very principles of 1789 which it was always attacking. The combination of archaic elements in its ideology and its lightning speed of advance in practice, belonged to the essence of fascism, to its 'pure paradox'. Then there was the military terminology, which had nothing to do with conservative thinking, such as soldier of labour, the battle of labour, commando. In direct opposition to the ideological principle of giving preference to the farmers and peasants, of *Blut und Boden* (blood and soil), during the Third Reich 700,000 farm labourers were moved into the cities to work in industry.

Mosse rightly points out the importance of making a clear distinction between fascist and reactionary regimes. Thus many people refer to Mussolini's dictatorship as an *Entwicklungsdiktatur*, thus expressing an enthusiasm not found in highly industrialized countries for everything to do with industry and technology, and also the suspicion that any society undergoing rapid industrial expansion may develop fascist tendencies. In 1968 the American historian, David Schoenbaum, in his book *Hitler's Social Revolution : Class and Status in Nazi Germany 1933–1939* pointed out that by 1939 many things had happened that Hitler had not promised. The towns had grown, the concentration of capital had increased, the number of people living in the country had decreased, more and more women were working in offices and factories, the gap between the rich and the poor had grown larger, the proportion of the gross national product taken up by industry had increased, and that taken up by agriculture decreased. Industrial workers were relatively well off, the 'independent businessmen' were less well off, for the department stores had merely been 'Aryanized' and not abolished. The gulf between the theoretical programme and its implementation was very wide.

Fascism and the christian churches

If we can't be holy men, we can at least be heroes.
YOUNG ITALIAN FASCIST, 1930

When the German Chancellor Brüning visited the then Cardinal Secretary of State (later Pope) Pacelli, while he was making a state visit to Rome in the summer of 1931, Pacelli urged him to form a right-wing government which would include the National Socialists, in order that he might then achieve his much desired concordat. The Chancellor told him that he was totally mistaken about the character of the NSDAP, which was neither religious nor tolerant. This conversation shows the ambivalence in the relationship between the Church and fascism. All the Church was interested in was securing the concordat and thus its rights. What it liked about the fascisms was that they did not believe in the 'hideous fetishes of liberalism'. When Mussolini signed the Lateran Treaty in 1929 he appeared to the Pope as if sent by Providence. However, only a few months later, he declared that the Christian religion would have remained one of the many Jewish sects, had its influence not reached Imperial Rome. He was, as Ciano said, both Catholic and anti-Christian. He admired the Church's Roman organization, but was totally indifferent to its religious significance. In 1930 a leading fascist referred to early Christianity as a matter of the Jews, and as a kind of mystical bolshevism, while the Catholic

Church was 'una cosa romana'. Of course the Pope was obliged to condemn these remarks as heretical. But the Church did not dare to fall out with the fascists, even when at the beginning of 1931 they began to take measures against the Catholic action movement and the Catholic youth organizations. The Church's attitude continued until 1945, for it was afraid of losing the support of powers so active in the battle against the forces that it hated – liberalism and democracy. The Church regarded the *Risorgimento* as a rather larger version of the 'Fiume adventure'. Also the ties linking both fascism and the Church with the middle class and the agrarian population led to certain common attitudes and actions.

As long as religion was 'positive', that is, as long as it recognized and supported the state, it could rely on the help of the state in its own endeavours. But the fascist party began to assume its own ecclesiastic character, *ecclesiasticità*, and this led to a kind of 'love-hatred' between the two institutions.

Hitler greeting *Reichsbischof* Müller and the Roman Catholic abbot Schachleitner, official guests at the Nuremberg rally. The *Reichsbischof* was made supreme head of the German protestant church to create and preside over a Nazi brand of Christianity. Opposition to him crystallized in the fundamentalist 'Confessional Church' whose best-known representative, Pastor Niemöller, was imprisoned in a concentration camp.

Metropolitan State University
Library Services

Both dictators, Hitler as well as Mussolini, admired the Catholic Church as an organization and sought to emulate it, but they rejected the Church's claim to leadership and ultimate authority, just as the early fascisms had rejected the Church and had demanded the expropriation of church property. This extreme view was put too by Mussolini after he had joined forces with the ruling classes and thus also with the Church. The National Socialists did not want to tolerate any Church other than themselves either. They believed that once they had got rid of the priests and the Church organizations, there would be no more Christianity. The war inhibited this development because they had to take into consideration the opinion of large sections of the population. Ideologically, Italian fascism was anti-Christian and heathen. Rocco, a descendant of nationalism and vigorously opposed to the liberal Gentile, resorted in his arguments against liberalism to the Catholic political philosophy that had been developed in the battle against the ideas of the French revolution. Barnes's *The Universal Aspects of Fascism*, which was published in 1928 with an introduction by Mussolini, interpreted fascism according to the view of the French neo-scholastic philosopher, Maritain, as a Catholic theocracy. The Church could remain, as Evola remarked during that same year, as long as it was willing to subordinate itself to the Empire. Fascism borrowed some of its ethical concepts from the Church, such as nation and family. In its view the Church in Italy should be tolerated as a civil religion and *instrumentum regni*, but basically fascism hoped to reawaken the vitality of the Roman heathen tradition.

Hitler had still promised to protect 'positive' Christianity in the elections of early 1933. What he meant by positive was a Christianity as understood by National Socialists: Jesus could not have been a Jew but was elevated into an Aryan demigod. Otherwise the Church had to serve the interests of Germany; the organization of 'German Christians' and the appointment of a *Reichsbischof* for all the evangelical Churches led to a major conflict between

the National Socialist state and the Churches. There
were certain tendencies in the party which believed
in taking up the battle with the Churches. For
them Hitler himself became a demigod, a radiant
being: 'It is as if God were coming to you', wrote
the SS newspaper, *Das Schwarze Korps*, in 1941.
This kind of anti-Christian 'faith' became wide-
spread, as did the belief that the time had come to
put an end to the poisonous effect of Christianity.
In 1935 Hitler expressed the view that one Christian
sect was as bad as another. In 1941 he declared that
the great purpose of National Socialism was the
solution of the 'problem of the Churches'. He himself, he assured his audience, had always been a
heathen.

We can rightly assume then that the National
Socialists' hostility towards the Roman Catholic
Church was part and parcel of their nationalist
ideology. They saw the Church, in the words of
General Ludendorff, as an *überstaatliche Macht*, a
power transcending that of the state. In his *Decline
of the West* Spengler had called it one of the 'pro-

At the conclusion of
the Concordat
meeting in Rome in
1933. Seated second
from the right is Vice-
Chancellor von Papen
with Cardinal Pacelli,
later Pope Pius XII, at
the head of the table.
Standing on the far
right is secretary of
state, Cardinal
Montini — the present
Pope Paul VI.

Metropolitan State University
Library Services

letarian religions' which had opposed the new Caesars. The problems created by the fascists' opposition to the Church were far greater in Germany than in Italy. Even if many early Italian fascists were hostile to the Church, Evola, their ideologist, still remained an outsider, whereas Alfred Rosenberg, the National Socialists' main opponent of the Church, was editor-in-chief of their most important paper, the *Völkischer Beobachter*. Even when Pope Pius XI came out against the new heathenism in Germany in his encyclical, 'With growing anxiety', the Vatican was most careful to avoid severing its links with the Third Reich. Their mutual hatred of democracy and liberalism was more important to the Church than the fascists' hostility towards itself.

In our examination of the relationship between the Churches and the fascist powers we must also bear in mind that there were numerous movements which were either fascist, or inclined towards fascism, that were on good terms with the Church – that is, with the exception of the Russian fascists, to the Roman Catholic Church. The Austria of Dollfuss and Schuschnigg even produced the concept of 'clerico-fascism' as a specific form of European fascism. Codreanu's movement in Rumania was an extreme example of this, for he saw himself as a Christlike figure, as a man invested with a mystic authority. The names of his first movements are proof of this, the 'Brotherhood of the Cross' and the 'Legion of the Archangel Michael'. His aim was more a theology of the cross inspired by the belief in the union in death with the spirit of the *Volk*. The small groups of his Iron Guard were the 'death commando', whose battle cry was 'Long live death, long live the Legion and the Captain, the Captain!'

Ante Pavelić's Ustasha movement, which was the only fascist movement in the Balkans to come to power during the war, in 1941, had also begun as a nationalist, revolutionary and terrorist secret society. It stood for a mystic belief in the power of *Volkstum* in opposition to the Pan-Serbian, orthodox nationalism of Belgrade. It attacked indiscriminately free-

The meeting in Venice, December 1941, between the Italian Foreign Minister, Count Ciano, and here, Ante Pavelić, the self-styled *Poglavnik 'Führer'* of Croatia.

masons, Jews, liberals and bolsheviks, and had close ties with the Roman Catholic Church. As Catholic Croats amounted to only fifty per cent of the population, but a homogeneous *völkisch* national state was being advocated, the strictly organized, authoritarian state soon developed into a regime of terror, with mass shootings, secret police and concentration camps. Even if the war had ended differently the state would scarcely have been viable. There were similar, though less radical, tendencies in the Slovak People's Party of Andrej Hlinka which organized the resistance of the Catholic peasant population of Slovakia to Czech attempts to centralize power in

Hlinka, who organized the resistance of the Slovak Catholic peasant population against Czech attempts to centralize power in Prague. The opposition of his successor, Tiso, and the post Munich (September 1938) government of truncated Czechoslovakia, led to the German take-over in March, 1939.

Prague, attempts which were condemned in Bratislava as Hussite and free-thinking. This was another example of extreme clerical fascism, where absolute authority was in the hands of a clergy whose aim was the renewal of the Slovak people in the Christian-conservative meaning of the word. Again the ties between this brand of fascism and pure fascism, especially that of Italy, were determined by their common rejection of any liberal democratic system.

Hlinka and Tiso wanted merely to achieve autonomy within the framework of Czechoslovakia, whereas the aim of the younger fascists under Tuka and his paramilitary 'Hlinka Guard' was complete separation from Prague, which was achieved, under pressure from Hitler, in March 1939. Anti-Semitism was particularly strong, since fifty per cent of the country's wealth in 1939 was in the hands of the Jewish, Hungarian-orientated minority. Persecution of the Jews was enforced during the war by the radical Propaganda Minister, Sano Mach. The fascist character of this persecution has been portrayed in Ladislav Grosman's *roman-à-clef*, *The Shop in the High Street*, which shows clearly how the 'Aryanizers' set about achieving their 'united Christian Europe'.

Russian fascism after 1917 also had a strictly religious character. It opposed atheist Soviet communism with 'Christian fascism' – its slogans were 'God, nation and labour'. Its first aim was to restore the Russian people to religion and the Orthodox Church. The situation was very different in Italy and Germany, as already described. The 'new nationalism' of the extreme right wing in the Weimar Republic after 1918, which was not National Socialist, had described the people as the bridge to God. 'Our destiny is the path of God and God is the nation', wrote Franz Schauwecker. In 1931 the Norwegian, Quisling, had tried to found a 'political and religious' party which would be based on Germanic concepts of God.

In 1790 Edmund Burke in his *Reflections on the French Revolution* referred with sarcasm to the 'political theologians' and the 'theological politicians' of his time. Similarly it soon became necessary for the fascists to progress a step further beyond their anti-Christian attitude and to search for an '*ersatz religion*' for the masses, in the Sorelian sense. At first they contented themselves with borrowing merely the outward ecclesiastical forms without the content. These included the constant repetition of certain formulae, slogans and symbols, all designed to give fascism the appearance of a 'religion of the fatherland'. Similarly they imitated the hierarchical structure and authoritarian attitude of the Catholic Church. While claiming to have created something quite new, and to have made a new beginning, they were in fact only playing with the old symbols and forms of the Christian Churches. When Mussolini, in his first parliamentary speech after his take-over in 1922, asked God to help him, he deliberately made use of 'this renewal', as he expressed it, as a weapon against the socialist and liberal agnostics, in order to make the Italians into better citizens by urging them to fulfil their duty to God. On the basis of modern agnosticism they wanted to exploit traditional values in order to create a new, heathen faith. The fascists were interested in all the different deviations that had developed in the history of the official Church. Mussolini called his early movement a 'Church of heresies', and the SS devoted itself to an exhaustive study of the medieval heretical movements.

Dr Josef Tiso, who was to be the President of satellite Slovakia.

Friedrich Heer offers some interesting examples of this transformed racialist and *völkisch* Christian philosophy in his book *Der Glaube des Adolf Hitler* (1968). This development resulted ultimately in the creation of neo-heathen ideas, in Italy with links going back to ancient Rome, and in Germany with ancient Germanic faiths. Although Hitler showed little interest in such matters at first, he sanctioned Himmler's attempts to establish an 'experimental religion' with his *Ahnenerbe* (the SS research institution into Germany's 'ancestral heritage'). He believed that Christianity had poisoned the soul of the Nordic race and therefore turned to the cult of ancestors and the mythology of antiquity. There was, of course, little clarity about the direction this would take. Hitler became enthusiastic about the theory of glacial cosmogony which had been developed by the Austrian engineer Hörbiger, while Himmler remained fascinated by the occult and by astrology. They saw themselves, as Himmler expressed it in his 'eternal marching orders' of 1936, as the ancestors of the future, immortal Germanic races. The fascists' outward resemblance to the traditionalists of various kinds, as suggested by Lipset, created the basis for an extreme, demonological *Weltanschauung*.

Fascism and the intellectuals

*The true paradises
are those which one has
already lost.*

MARCEL PROUST

Although European fascism was a predominantly middle-class movement it is not true to say that the bourgeois intellectuals were particularly susceptible to fascism. Most of the left-wing intellectuals in Italy and Germany chose to emigrate, particularly if they were Jews who were persecuted anyway on account of their race. There were also many writers, especially in Germany, who took refuge in 'inner emigration', or those who sought an even greater safety, as Ernst Jünger and Gottfried Benn, in the Prussian army.

Nevertheless, we can not ignore the fact that there were many European intellectuals who became dedicated to fascism out of genuine conviction, and who defended it to the bitter end. These included the German philosopher Martin Heidegger, the Italian philosopher Gentile, the American poet Ezra Pound, the German poet Gottfried Benn and the Norwegian poet Knud Hamsun. Writers in English who are regarded as having some affinity with fascism include the novelists D. H. Lawrence, Wyndham Lewis and Henry Williamson, and the poets Roy Campbell and W. B. Yeats. Some of these are discussed in John Harrison's book *The Reactionaries* (1966). There is an enormous amount of material concerning the intellectual world of these people, which has not yet been exposed to a thorough examination.

Basically it can be said that these men did not come to fascism because they were reactionaries, but because they judged the present by traditional, archaic standards, and thus became revolutionaries. Mosley maintains that no writer can be both a fascist and a reactionary at the same time. A right-wing movement has nothing to do with fascism, which is revolutionary but not reactionary. Those poets and philosophers, by accepting fascism, certainly made a political decision and were taking a political responsibility upon themselves. Where they were mistaken was in believing that they had anything to say politically, whereas in fact they were merely backward-looking prophets.

One must bear in mind that many philosophers and writers were justifiably critical of certain contemporary developments, without necessarily tending towards fascism. Thus in Spain Ortega y Gasset and Miguel de Unamuno declared in 1933 that the Spanish Republic had not come up to their expectations. Unamuno was exiled (1924–30) for opposing

Harold Nicolson who briefly edited Mosley's new party newspaper. However when Mosley openly embraced fascism, he parted company with him.

Ezra Pound, the 72-year-old poet, after his release from the mental asylum in Washington to which the American government had confined him for his anti-American propaganda broadcasts during World War II.

the dictatorship of General Primo de Rivera, and Ortega emigrated to Portugal from 1936 to 1949. Neither of them can be accused of being a fascist because of their criticism of parliamentary socialist democracy in Spain. Similarly, Harold Nicolson, who for a time edited Mosley's newspaper, watched Mussolini speaking from a balcony of his palace in Rome, but was disgusted and did not follow Mosley when he became an extreme fascist because he wanted to see the respectability of the English middle classes maintained in the New Party.

What about the writers who became convinced fascists? Ezra Pound and Knud Hamsun in particular supported fascism until the end and even after that. Pound, a distinguished lyric poet, lived in Italy for many years. As early as 1926 he had praised Mussolini,

maintaining that he was far superior to the last three
American Presidents and British Prime Ministers.
He explained that if the intellectuals tended to reject
him, it did not mean anything, for they knew nothing
about the state, about government or economic
matters. They had not cared for Henry Ford, either,
and he had given his workers the five-day week
without indulging in any theories. Pound was
fascinated by all aspects of politics but, like Hamsun,
was primarily concerned for the well-being of his
own people. He admired Thomas Jefferson, and in
1933 wrote *Jefferson and/or Mussolini*, which was
not published until 1935 after having been rejected
by forty publishers. His conception of history was
derived from the American historian, Brooks Adams,
brother of the President. Like Mosca and Pareto,
Adams distinguished between the imaginative and
the economic human type. The interplay between
the two, in his view, determined the course of human
history. Like Vico, Adams saw history as a cycle of
constantly changing civilizations, caught in a spiral
of rise and fall. Pound often referred to the cultural
circulation theory Leo Frobenius had outlined in his
book *Schicksalskunde im Sinne des Kulturwerdens*
(1932). According to this theory each culture goes
through the process of preparation and development,
followed by adaptation and finally the period of
specialization which is the beginning of the end.
Frobenius viewed the outbreak of the world economic
crisis as such an end, heralding a new era in human
history.

Thus Pound became interested in finding economic
solutions which would benefit the whole people.
Inspired by the 'populist' movement which had had
a large following for a time in the nineteenth century
among the American farmers who were weighed down
by debts, he came across the economic theories of
Silvio Gesell (1862–1930), whose main work, *Natür-
liche Wirtschaftsordnung durch Freiland und Freigeld*,
was published in 1911, and who in 1919 became
Finance Minister of the Bavarian *Räterepublik*.
Pound, influenced by these ideas, and by his contempt for the world of international finance, came

Metropolitan State University
Library Services

to admire Mussolini's creation of the corporate
state. He had few direct contacts with fascism. He
spoke to Mussolini only once, when he thanked
him on receiving a prize for his study of Cavalcanti,
who had been a friend of Dante. Mussolini was
disappointed that Pound did not discuss poetry
with him, insisting instead on outlining his monetary
theories.

Pound was in no way an anti-communist but, in
contrast to Lenin and the Russian bolsheviks, he
had little confidence in the European and American
communists. The only Germans he respected were
Gesell and Frobenius. He rejected Nietzsche's will
to power as the ideas of an 'ill-balanced, hysterical
teuto-pollak'. He rejected Hitler too. In 1933 he
wrote that fascism could be achieved without the
parades and without Hitler's shouting, although in
Rapallo he assiduously ignored the same phenomena
in Mussolini's Italy. What he admired in Italian
fascism was the precedence given to production
over distribution, 'the battle of the grain', for he
scorned tradesmen and the apparent rejection of the
whole concept of factories, in line with Jefferson and
the 'Anti-snob movement'. Clearly his political
Weltanschauung was very limited and prejudiced,
but he can hardly be described as a fascist. The
poet's downfall was caused by the broadcasts he
made on the Italian radio, which led to his long and
degrading imprisonment in the American prisoner-
of-war camp at Pisa and his being taken to a mental
hospital after his trial.

The Norwegian poet Knud Hamsun also began
as a nationalist. But his attitude to the world was
totally different from that of the American. He was
inspired by Nietzsche's supermen and Dostoievsky's
'great terrorists'. Significantly, his works have had
their greatest success in Germany and the USSR.
In his works his characters live in a heathen nature
inhabited by gods. As a young man he had had
anarchist tendencies and in the battle for the
separation of Norway from Sweden he showed left-
wing nationalist views. After that he became a
moderate conservative, solely concerned about the

Nobel prize winning
novelist, Norwegian
Knud Hamsun.
Always an ardent
admirer of Germany,
he collaborated with
the Nazis during
World War II.

greatness of Norway and its liberation from its economic dependence on Britain, and the struggle to prevent the 'Swissification' of the country. He soon became anti-liberal and anti-socialist. Liberalism, he wrote in 1895, had introduced the old, unnatural, mistaken idea 'that the five-foot masses should elect their six-foot leaders'. He despised the masses and admired both the aristocrats and the adventurers. He struggled against the anonymity of modern society, against banks, big industry, the unions and the press. These firmly held prejudices were the cause of his antipathy towards England and his admiration for Germany, which remained unshaken. On 7 May 1945 he wrote an obituary of Hitler in Quisling's newspaper, *Aftenposten*, paying homage to him as a great reformer who had lived 'in an era of unparalleled savagery' and who had eventually fallen victim to it. By then Hamsun was nearly eighty-six, almost totally deaf and isolated from his

Gottfried Benn, doctor of medicine and lyric poet whose elitist view of the world made him an early admirer of the Nazi revolution. Its vulgar reality, however, offended his moral and aesthetic sensibilities and turned him into a disillusioned and disaffected onlooker.

family, but his mental faculties were still unimpaired, as his memoirs of his internment and trial, published in 1948, show. His main concern was for the greatness of Norway, which he thought might be achieved by his country's union with the Third Reich. Like Pound, he was never a party man, and was neither right- nor left-wing. Sten Sparre Nilson pointed out that the English were for Hamsun what the Jews were for Hitler – the incarnation of absolute evil. Even in 1914 he was anti-British and pro-German because England stood in the way of Germany's expansion overseas. His sense of national justice was pleased when the National Socialists came to power in 1933, believing as he did that they would give Germany the strength to confront England successfully, although he saw the fundamental reasons for the conflict between Britain and Germany more clearly than Hitler did. He was not conversant with the ideas of the National Socialists, nor did they interest him, any more than did Quisling's, whom he never saw. He was neither an anti-Semite nor an opponent of the Soviet Union, although he never admitted this in public. He condemned the Norwegian resistance as pointless, although in many cases he pleaded with the German authorities on behalf of those who were condemned, and was sometimes successful. The Germans finally began to find his ideas a nuisance – an extreme example of this is given in the protocol of the conversation between Hamsun and Hitler in the summer of 1943, which was published by Nilson. Hamsun interrupted Hitler's flow of speech several times, in order to talk about Norway's shipping industry or to complain about the *Preusserei* (Prussianism) of the German Commissar Terboven, whom he believed to be destroying more than Hitler could create. Hamsun was obsessed by the idea of Pan-Germanism, and the belief in the inherent superiority of the Nordic race, which in his prejudiced view did not include the British. They were western and democratic, and thus, for him, degraded.

In 1950 Benn published a work of self-justification under the title *Doppelleben* ('Double Life'). In it he described Hamsun's memoirs as 'sweet and silly, like so many of his books', and pointed out that the reader is left ignorant of the political context. However, when one reads what Benn himself wrote after 1933 in order to please the National Socialist regime, it is hard to escape the conclusion that his own criticism of Hamsun is scarcely justified.

Thought is cynical; it takes place mainly in Berlin. We recommend the *Weserlied* (Song of the Weser) to take its place.

GOTTFRIED BENN, 1934

Oswald Spengler whose *Decline of the West* popularized an elitist anti-democratic conception of history. Although an extreme right-wing conservative, he was not a Nazi and cautiously criticized their ideology after they assumed power.

Benn was one of the leading Expressionist writers in Germany during the time of the Weimar Republic, and he saw the events of 1933 as heralding a turning point in the history of the German people. An admirer of Nietzsche, Spengler and Frobenius, this cool sceptic viewed the world as an aesthetic problem. As a doctor he was fascinated by the problems of breeding and the life style of a great nation. Primitive feeling was in his view the last reserve of European man. He believed that the people would take over as the leaders, for they were best suited to do so, according to the 'law of vitality' in the 'age of breeding'. The breed must be safeguarded against degeneration and emasculation. In 1933 he really believed that a genuine renewal of the German people would provide an escape from rationalism, functionalism and the paralysis of civilization. But he soon had doubts; his references to most Germans as members of an exhausted people cannot have sounded very good to Nazi ears. He spoke in radical terms of 'elimination and breeding', but stressed that such matters should only be treated in deadly earnest, for they were 'lethal'.

During the war Benn was sent to lonely garrison towns in east Germany, after the *Reichsschrifttums-kammer* had banned him from further writing in 1938. In his isolation Benn poured out the despair in his soul through his writings. He pointed to the mystic wholeness of fools, the collective experience possessed by those who, as individuals, had little experience. Hegel had regarded Napoleon as the embodiment of the world spirit, but had been horrified by the sight of the plundering French grenadiers. Similarly, Benn, after years of writing about the founding of a new and heroic feeling of life which would be full of sacrifice, now complained in Warthegau in 1943 about the poor food, the 'barrack bread', the *ersatz* honey, cabbage soup and potatoes.

His self-justification of 1950 tries to over-simplify. He writes, for instance, that there was no concept of political emigration in Germany before 1933, thus conveniently forgetting the 'forty-eighters' after 1848 and the socialists after Bismarck's anti-socialist legislation, and claims that the government had come to power 'legally', which is largely true, but is not sufficient to justify his political attitude. He writes that nobody took the Nazi programme of racialism and anti-Semitism seriously in 1933 – it was only later that the horrifying truth began to dawn on people. He now realized once again that the poet had no place in the political scene, needing solitude, asceticism and a monklike existence in order to create. In 1934 Benn, in a review of Evola's book *Revolt against the Modern World*, suggested that Europe could only be saved by a new kind of monastic life, through elitism, asceticism and fasting. 'This is how we were, and this is how we shall be again.'

The political attitudes of D. H. Lawrence cannot be looked at in isolation from the spirit of the times in his country and in Europe. There were no well-organized reactionary movements in England at the turn of the century as there were in France and Germany. Popular hostility to immigrants from Europe was partly inspired by anti-Semitism, as too was some of the pro-Boer sentiment, while opposition to the principle of parliamentary democracy was led by the imperialist, Milner. As a writer Lawrence was always in search of a perfect world, an ideal society. He admired Nietzsche, Jung, Dacqué and Frobenius. This led him back to the medium of the fairy story and to myth. Lawrence was fascinated by the primitive; he admired the

Dezso Szabo, a brilliant propagandist who edited his own newspaper *Life and Literature* and whose anti-semitic and nationalist views impressed Hungary's intellectuals and young officers.

Celts and the Germanic tribes and the life of simple people who had no contact with modern civilization. This was what fascinated him about Mexico, where he lived for a long time. His plan to set up colonies of like-minded people was not a success. Searching, like Nietzsche, for an unknown god he portrayed man in his novels as an animal, following its own instincts. The driving forces in life were love and the will to power. Like Pound and Hamsun he longed for a dictator, a charismatic leader who would bring the people a new currency, a just society and new towns. Lawrence's theories contained a certain amount of racialism, of death symbolism and the veneration of the warrior as the great man of action. Basically his ideas had some affinity with those expressed in modern philosophy after Bergson. At heart he was a poet and did not care much about politics. He was certainly not a Christian, but rather a heathen in the sense of the ancient classics. Nor was he a fascist in the political sense; at most he might be said to have had anarchist tendencies.

Writers who concern themselves with politics soon find that they are in danger of becoming politically stereotyped. An example of this is the Hungarian writer, Deszo Szabó (1879–1945), who by 1914 was expressing ideas which were close to those of Nietzsche and modern irrationalism and nationalism. He was a brilliant propagandist and edited his own newspaper, *Leben und Literatur*, in which he developed a new Hungarian ideology which was neither left- nor right-wing and which had a great influence on the young intellectuals and officers. By 1923 he had become anti-Semitic, but for purely nationalist and not racialist reasons. He rejected German National Socialism and was suspicious of the powerful influence of the German minority in Hungary. He advocated the amalgamation of nationalism and socialism under the leadership of the middle classes. He opposed the counter-revolutionary regime of Horthy and was critical of the Church. For this reason he was unable to be the ideologist of the Arrow Cross party.

No one has yet written a book about the European

Metropolitan State University
Library Services

intellectuals and their relationship to fascism. It would be incorrect to make too facile an equation and label every writer who showed fascist tendencies (either for a time or up until the end) as a fascist. Just as one can only speak of the existence of fascism when all its distinguishing factors are present, one can only speak of fascists when they exhibit all these elements together. This cannot be said of any of the above mentioned writers, although it should be borne in mind that, by publicly supporting fascist regimes, they helped them.

A mass movement of the discontented

As already mentioned, many European intellectuals were dissatisfied with the political situation in their own country as well as in the world – in short, with the entire human situation. They found their feelings of discontent echoed in the *Kulturpessimismus* of many nineteenth-century philosophers, in Bergson and finally in the Expressionists' reaction to life and the beginnings of existentialism. Although many of them, like the German philosopher Martin Heidegger, or Gentile, imagined that fascism would be a means to bring about change and improvement, and therefore welcomed it, their arguments would never have brought fascism to power. This was achieved by the support of a whole social class, the lower middle class and the so-called new middle class. The lower middle classes, above all the small 'independent' shopkeeper, the enemy of the big concerns, was backward-looking, and was ultimately disappointed with fascism. The new middle class, on the other hand, such as civil servants or executives in industry, engineers, technocrats and managers, all of whom were more important in the world of industrial capitalism than the actual financiers, were, whatever their political persuasion, always in favour of progress. They were concerned for the future of modern industrial society.

As early as 1913 the French sociologist André Siegfried pointed out that the chauvinist movements in France between 1871 and 1914 were based largely on the *petit bourgeoisie*, which felt hopelessly hemmed in between the upper classes who were in control of finance and industry and the organized workers. They felt increasingly threatened, both mentally and physically, in a world of rationalized production which they had to serve, but which they could neither understand nor influence. This feeling of fear became more extreme in the confusion following the First World War, and above all during the world economic crisis, and drove these sections of the population into the arms of the communists or the fascists. A small proportion of the bourgeois section of the so-called 'white-collar proletariat' went over to the left because they felt superior to the workers, no matter how desperate their own economic plight. Fascism seemed better suited to fulfil the needs of those who felt this way and who were filled with hostility towards the ruling circles. Of practically thirty parties which stood for election in Germany in 1932, almost fifty per cent based their appeal on middle class slogans. The hard core of the fascist parties was provided by social 'outsiders' – opportunists, upstarts and *arrivistes* who rejected the existing democratic society. In industry the *nouveaux riches* and the war profiteers were the first to go over to fascism in Italy and Germany, and not the old established leaders of industry.

In 1919–22 the Italian socialists showed little understanding for the demands and attitude of the soldiers returning home from the war. In 1929 the German trade unions showed a similar lack of sympathy for the unemployed. Thus the masses went over to fascism and helped to bring it to power. They both needed each other; the leaders of the fascist parties could not exist without the acclamation of the masses, and the masses acquired a feeling of certainty and security in life through the *Weltanschauung* and style of the fascist parties.

The mass of the people who up till then had been politically indifferent had become more restless as a result of the war and social upheavals, and now began to inundate the old, strictly organized parties and unions. These fluctuations in the middle class played an important part in the development of fascism throughout Europe. This displacement of social classes could be observed all over Europe after 1918. Laskó refers to the *demi-prolétaires plébéiens* in the Balkans. In fact it was not the big landowners in Italy who, as is often claimed, were the first to support fascism, but the average farmers in the Po valley and Romagna. Of course, fascism would never have come to power in Italy without the financial and moral support of the industrial and agricultural capitalists, but it will not do to underestimate the importance of the support from the lower middle class (shopkeepers of all kinds, middlemen, lease-hold farmers and small landowners). Workers too formed a not inconsiderable proportion of the fascist movement. In 1929 the membership of the union of agricultural workers sank from 800,000 to 300,000. Many workers in the docks and in the depressed shipping industry became fascist, encouraged too by the fact that Mussolini had worked with their trade union in 1919, when it had had strong anarchist tendencies.

Lipset has quite rightly pointed out that political extremism on the part of the middle class had origins which went back much further than the First World War, revolutions or the world economic crisis. There was the movement of the North American farmers which has already been mentioned; similar reactions were shown by the *Bund der Landwirte* (agricultural association) in Imperial Germany at the end of the nineteenth century. At the turn of the century there were many groups in Europe which were reactionary in their political and economic ideas but whose aims and methods were radical and extremist. Almost all of them became the germ cells of fascism. Why the 'uprooted' masses did not turn to left-wing extremism has been the subject of much discussion. Historians have spoken of the discrepancy or tension between the economic situation and the ideology of these classes. In 1933 Trotsky referred to the vast depths of 'darkness, ignorance and barbarism' in these sections of the population. He, together with Wilhelm Reich and Hendrik de Man, had become aware that this 'white-collar proletariat' was ideologically extremely anti-Marxist. The determination of the lower middle classes to remain bourgeois – on the one hand, in the face of the anti-bourgeois attitude of the politically organized proletariat, and on the other, despite the treatment they received at the hands of the property-owning bourgeoisie – meant political and economic suicide. Researchers such as Wilhelm Alff distinguish between the 'independent' middle class and the 'serving' middle class; the latter had always had fascist tendencies, while the former should have been more open to proletarian ideas. But even he must admit that people's political consciousness is not solely determined by their position in society. Nor should we forget that the communists only worked with other classes for purely tactical reasons. The fascists now took advantage of this communist *reservatio mentalis*, inevitably with great success.

National Socialism attracted many supporters from the ranks of the 'fifth Estate', the unemployed. One must bear in mind also that in Germany in 1932, of about 30,000,000 employed, only fifteen per cent were workers. Almost forty-five per cent consisted of the old and the new middle classes. There were vast differences between them, but they had in common a rapidly worsening economic plight and the growing threat of proletarianization. The ultra-cautious reformism of the Socialist Party and the extreme left, almost reckless programme of the Communist Party also drove some workers into the arms of the fascists. Many *Rotfrontkämpfer* (members of the communist fighting organization) joined the SA after their organization had been banned in 1929, and fought against their former comrades. 'Their motto was "It's quicker with them"', as one *émigré* communist wrote in 1933.

Also a high proportion of bourgeois liberal voters turned to the NSDAP. By 1933 the liberal parties in Germany had lost eighty per cent of their voters. During the period of the Weimar Republic their proportion of the poll sank from twenty-five per cent to three per cent. The Nazis themselves issued useful statistics relating to the proportion of various

Overleaf: At Nuremberg thousands of young members of Nazi organizations salute the *Führer* as he passes.

Reveille at a Hitler Youth camp. Considerable pressure was exercised to 'persuade' German youngsters to join the party's youth movement. Run on para-military lines it politically indoctrinated and physically prepared the youth for service in the armed forces.

professional groups in the membership of the NSDAP. They were taken in January 1920, September 1930 and in 1933, before and after the Nazi take-over. Apart from a few superficial fluctuations, the figures show a remarkable degree of consistency in the proportion of professional groups. The proportion of workers and employees stayed around thirty per cent, academics and students around twenty per cent, officials around twelve and a half per cent, white-collar workers around twenty per cent and peasants around ten per cent. Workers and peasants who, according to the name and the ideology of the party, should have provided the largest proportion of its members, in fact were not very well represented. National Socialism was a predominantly middle class movement, to a greater extent even than Italian fascism.

Thus a new type of politician appeared on the scene – one who sought 'secondary relations', and in so doing rejected the primary, i.e. the classical image of mankind, the Christian west and liberal democracy of the past two centuries. The Austrian writer Heimito von Doderer wrote in 1945 that people still did not realize that this turning away from European traditions, this denial of the individual, demanded a concept of the human being 'which up till then had only been applied to races of animals'. The individual human being was of little or no interest, becoming merely the object of racial calculations. Neither socialism nor communism had been able to overcome the real problem of modern man, the problem of alienation. This suggests yet another reason for the development and growth of fascism, and also helps to explain how people who were strongly individualistic, such as artists and poets, became supporters of fascism. Young people and dreamers flocked to the movement, not realizing that it was in reality being supported by forces which were in direct opposition to their own ideals. In 1928 Bonn, in the collection *Internationaler Faschismus*, pointed out that without the support of the

Below left: Hitler with Field Marshal Mannerheim, the grand old man of the conservative Finnish establishment. He won independence for Finland in 1920 after defeating native Red armies anxious to maintain the Soviet connection. As defence minister he built the famed Mannerheim Line. He was elected President in 1944 to negotiate, with the victorious Russians, Finland's withdrawal from the war.

Below right: Léon Degrelle leader of Belgium's pro-Nazi Rexists, who during the war commanded the Belgian contingent of the *Waffen SS*.

Danish volunteers of the *Waffen SS*.

big industrialists, fascism would never have grown so strong, but that those very industrialists were only interested in the mechanization of society. This was also valid for industrially under-developed areas such as the Balkans. There the task of this backward-looking ideology was to 'put an end to spiritual alienation as a first step towards improving economic conditions.'

Although fascist writers tended to despise the modern world without attempting to change it, and conjured up pictures of paradise lost, seeking to replace the traditional image of political man, *zoon politikon*, by 'natural' man who was purely creative in his thoughts and actions, fascism in fact, with its militarization, did much to encourage the development of modern industrial society. Fascist ideology glorified the three *Gestalten*, or original human types – the warrior, the peasant and the worker. It transformed German history into a mythology involving these three archetypes, and created a 'reactionary utopia' which had little to do with historical reality.

What fascist movements really wanted to breed, however, was a completely new human type, the 'political soldier' whose absolute devotion to action and willingness to sacrifice himself to the cause was not based on *Staatsraison*, but on political conviction. Here again it is clear that fascism treated ideology as the most important sphere of human activity. Thus we come to the second human pre-condition of fascism – in addition to the broad base of discontented sections of the population, fascism laid great store on the education of an elite which would be fanatically devoted to the movement and which by providing the hard core would guarantee some degree of permanence. These elites formed the new ruling class, the *Neuadel aus Blut und Boden* (new nobility of blood and soil). In Italy it was the fascist militia, and in Germany it was the SS. But in contrast to many National Socialist ideologists who tried to use historical examples to prove the importance of the fraternity of men, Himmler wanted to create a *Sippenorden* (order based on kin). The human counterpart was the inferior or sub-man whom they tried to 'destroy by work' in the concentration camps. The historical models were the Order of the Jesuits and the German *Ritterorden* (Order of Knights), that is, both totally masculine fraternities. All the European fascist movements had elites of this kind – the *Camelots du Roi* of the *Action Française*, the 'Blue Shirts' of the Portuguese National Syndicalists or the Spanish Falange. In spite of its attempts to win mass support, fascism was dominated by this concept of an elitist hierarchy.

The most interesting military fascist organization

was the 'Germanic' *Waffen-SS* which was deliberately regarded as supra-national and in a sense
as European. An ideology had to be created for it
which had nothing to do with Hitler's concept of
the Great German Empire and which condemned
the policies of the party leaders in the occupied
territories. Its adherents no longer acted for the
Führer and the party, but for the Reich. Like
Björnson and Hamsun they became obsessed with
the concept of Pan-Germanism. But the proportion
of Germanic volunteers from north and west Europe
in the whole of the *Waffen-SS* was very small. At
the beginning of 1945 it consisted of 910,000 men,
of whom 350,000 were non-German and of these
30,000 only were 'Germanic' volunteers.

The powerful state

An essential element in the fascist regimes and movements was their concept of the corporative state, as
realized mainly by Mussolini and those who
followed his example. In their search for something
to replace the parliamentary democracy they despised, they had discovered this mixture of revolutionary syndicalism and conservative, nationalist
convictions. It had come to public attention through
the lectures that Othmar Spann gave in Vienna in
the summer of 1920, *Der Wahre Staat, Vorlesungen
über Abbruch und Neubau der Gesellschaft* ('The
true state. Lectures on the destruction and rebuilding
of society'.) Catholic teaching on social questions
was also universalistic, in contrast to liberalism and
parliamentary democracy. An important element
in it was the concept of the 'organic', of natural
growth as opposed to that which is artificially
created. Italian fascism was strongly influenced
by the writings of Corradini, who wrote about 'the
regime of the productive bourgeoisie' and suggested
dividing up the nation into syndicates. By 1919 the
Associazione Nationalista Italiana had emphasized
the idea of syndicates, of Estates, for it had realized
that the principles of collectivity and inner discipline
were important for the workers' movement.

In his election campaign in the autumn of 1919,

Mussolini demanded representation in an official council for the professions, for intellectual and manual work, industry, commerce and agriculture. Similar tendencies could be seen in the revolution in Germany in 1918–19, where left-wing radicals and conservatives resembled each other in their concept of society being organized on the basis of professions in the *Rätesystem* (system of workers' councils). Richard von Moellendorf, who in 1918 was a conservative Under-Secretary of State in the German Economic Ministry, under a socialist minister, called this 'organizational socialism'. He wanted to set up a 'people's economic council' which would direct the 'basic economy'. But the Social Democrats' fear of nationalizing the industries producing raw materials prevented his plans from being realized. His ideas were developed further during the Weimar period by the nationalists as 'Prussian socialism'.

Herman Heller, who in 1931 wrote a highly critical, but at the same time objective, analysis of Italian fascism, and who rejected it totally as a *Weltanschauung* because of its negative and restorative attitude, remarked nevertheless that the fascist concept of the corporative state was fascinating for Europe. 'The class problem is indeed the crucial point.' Only if the Italian dictatorship in the form of the corporative state managed to overcome the crisis of the class state would it be justified. The problem lay in the fact that the corporative state would have to set up an autarky, a self-sufficient economy, and Italy was dependent on her relations with the world economy, because of her lack of raw materials and hard currency.

In theory fascism appeared to be a combination of nationalism and socialism. In practice, socialism was suppressed by nationalism. Wages were pegged, strikes were banned, workers were not allowed to change their places of work freely and were made virtually into the slaves of a state-protected economy. Italy probably provided the most unfavourable conditions for a positive realization of the corporate state and economy, in addition to which she was hard hit by the world economic crisis. The corporative legislation of 1926 did not correspond to the high ideals of which the fascists had boasted. Employers and employees were separated, and the central workers' syndicate was abolished because of pressure from the employers. By 1931, five years after the law had been passed, there still was not one single corporation in existence, only the ministry and the National Council of Corporations, which in practice were merely state organs and 'institutions of a centralist dictatorship' for the purpose of controlling the workers. The same purpose was served by the *Dopolavoro* ('after work'), whose aims and functions corresponded to the German organization of the *Arbeitsfront, Kraft durch Freude* (strength through joy), which organized sporting, theatrical and musical events, excursions and similar forms of non-political entertainment. What was happening in practice was the centralist, dictatorial de-politicization of the entire Italian people.

The whole of Europe looked on with interest to see how this experiment worked out, hoping that if it were successful it would provide a model for overcoming the difficulties in the capitalist system. It is astonishing how many European fascist movements included the corporative and organic theory of the state in their programme, even groups which had adopted fundamentally National Socialist principles. The corporative and organic theory of the state formed an important part of the programmes of the fascist movements in Great Britain, Belgium, France, the Netherlands and Norway. The Flemish *Verbond van Dietsche Nationaalsolidaristen*, which was mainly German-orientated, still aimed at creating the one 'organic' Germanic state with a corporate economy. The Walloon movements in Belgium were also in favour of the corporate system.

The socialism which had provided Mussolini's political origins soon lost all significance in the fascist state. By 1924 it was laid down that the fundamental principle of syndicalism was the protection of property. So fascism developed into a dictatorship in a form which was adapted to the requirements of capitalist society. Even the German nationalist jurist Ludwig Bernhard referred in 1924 in his book *Das System Mussolini* to fascist corporativism as a 'police system masquerading as an attempt to create a government based on representation of the professions'.

Certainly the war economy of 1914–18, with state control and intervention, must have provided a model for fascism, in contrast to the free market economy and liberal *laissez faire*. But just as the symbol of Roman fascism, the fasces, was not an 'organically' grown tree trunk, but a bundle of roots forcibly pressed together, so too the fascist state did not grow organically, and was even less of an organic structure. The property-owning bourgeoisie and the state took the profits, the working people paid the bill. The overcoming of the class struggle and the introduction of social justice remained in the programmes of the fascist movements, but were never realized.

German National Socialism, in contrast to Italian fascism which extolled the state, put forward the concept of 'German socialism'. It demanded that the people work in the service of the community and at the same time set the party as the highest authority over industry. The entrepreneur was not prevented from earning, but what he did was determined by the authority of the party and the state. National Socialism took 'its own pure idea', as Hitler explained in 1934, from two opposing camps, private, bourgeois society and the socialist state. The *Volksgemeinschaft* was proclaimed as embracing all the interests of the whole nation. In contrast to the mechanically organized mass of liberal and socialist societies, it would create organic professions, such as the military profession, or the peasantry or labouring class to form an 'organic *Stände-Nation*'. It did not want fundamental or revolutionary changes in the social structure of Germany. It set out to achieve a classless society on a national, not socialist, basis. Economic concepts were militarized. The entrepreneur became an 'officer of industry'. It spoke of 'soldiers of work'. The mythology of the front in the First World War was transferred to the structure of the German economy, an ideological attitude which was considerably fortified after 1936 with the intensified rearmament programme, and then in the Second World War.

The manner in which National Socialist state law interpreted this development is significant. The class struggle, which merely served the interests of 'the Jew', was replaced by an organic structuring of the entire people into professions, *Berufsgemeinschaften und Berufsstände,* all of which were organized on a strictly hierarchical basis, with flags and uniforms. These *Stände* had no political function, serving merely to provide a certain amount of self-administration in the handling of certain aspects of professional life. All political power was in the hands of the party leadership which 'acted solely in the interests of the national community'. The *Reichs-nährstand* (the Reich Agricultural Estate) and *Reichskulturkammer* (Reich Board of Arts and Culture) were thus also *Stände,* although the organization which succeeded the socialist and Christian trade unions, the *Deutsche Arbeitsfront* (German Labour Front), was not.

The driving forces of fascism

Thus far discussion has been confined to the historical pre-conditions and the 'elements' of fascism. These included its ideology or *Weltanschauung*, but from what sources did it spring? We shall now examine the ideological and spiritual 'driving forces', always bearing in mind that the historical pre-conditions of fascism were, are and always will be extremely varied, although having some essential characteristics in common. The elements and driving forces that have been named so far include a radical nationalism which often enough develops into imperialism; an equally extreme form of militarism; an extreme racialism which usually appears in the form of anti-Semitism; the use of terror as a principle in internal and foreign affairs; totalitarianism as a political and social order; and finally the authoritarian *Führerprinzip*. Let us now examine these driving forces of fascism from a structural-analytical and historical point of view.

Das Gros eines Volkes vermittelt nur eine animalische Botschaft, keine geistige. (The bulk of a people conveys only an animalistic message, not a spiritual one.)

CLAIRE GOLL

We have seen how, from the end of the last century, people had been driven by an inner sense of void, by the nihilism of modern man, from the lack of social or religious ties brought about by atheism, into activism merely for its own sake, irrespective of its aims and purpose. Mussolini clung to a kind of vague '*mistico dell' azione*', before the amalgamation with Corradini's Nationalists provided him with a rational, though nationalist, *Staatsraison*. It was not without reason that fascism was based on the modern 'life philosophy' of 'Bergsonism', according to which existence is engendered by the creative *élan*, and contemplation is 'absorbed' in action. For the mystic, the message of Bergson was that man should be radically 're-formed'. Thus the principle uniting socialism and fascism, and fascism's fundamental opposition to conservatism, becomes evident. We should not be misled by the pessimism and death symbolism, which are common to them both. It is not without significance that in certain respects fascism originated among youth movements. The figure of the peasant was mythologized as an eternal symbol of the people, but the fascists turned to the young people of the cities for political action. When in 1921 Hitler selected twenty-five men as a body-guard, forming the core of the future SA, fifteen of them were under twenty. In January 1933, immediately before the seizure of power, over forty per cent of party members were between twenty-one and thirty years old, only twenty-eight per cent aged between thirty and forty and only seventeen per cent were over forty.

The young were regarded by all the fascist movements as guarantors of the future. In Italy they had their own anthem, the *Giovanezza*. National Socialism took over Moeller van den Bruck's *Das Recht der jungen Völker* (1919). This German nationalist was clearly aware that 'in itself' no people was either 'young or old'. The youth of a people was determined by whether it was prepared for action, to expand to make room for its growing population. The ideas of Darwin and Nietzsche lay behind this view. The young people of the nation should also be the means of breeding a 'new' type of human being – something of which the older generation was neither willing nor capable. It is very interesting that the fascists themselves, who, as we have seen, thought along cyclical lines, themselves began to fall victim to this changing cycle of elites. In Italy the young men 'of the class of 35' began to turn against the party establishment and, reflecting the beginnings of fascism, forged ahead to the very extremes of the political movement. George L. Mosse rightly points out that, but for the war, Hitler would soon have had difficulties with the SS, 'which was more concerned with the power of the will than with ideology'.

Their strange passion for marching was another reflection of the activism of the 'life philosophy', the preference given to instinct over reason, to action rather than calculation. 'Marching is more important than studying', the students in the Third Reich were taught, and in 1936 Himmler issued the SS with his famous 'eternal marching orders'. D'Annunzio's march on Fiume and Horthy's march on Budapest in 1919 were followed by the march on Rome in 1922, the proposed march on Berlin in 1923, the marches of the rebel troops on Warsaw and Lisbon in May 1926, the march on Helsinki in 1930, and the march on Vienna by the Carinthian *Heimwehr* in September 1931. Hans Frank, the Governor-General of Poland, wrote in prison at Nuremberg in 1946 that at the Reich Party rallies nobody had given any thought to ideology, programmes or politics. Hitler's person had dominated everything. Whatever he said determined future events. He could have changed their whole ideology if he had wanted. Wildly applauding, they would have granted him anything. 'If he had for example suddenly proclaimed their friendship with the Jews, it would have been accepted.'

Nationalism

Politics is the national cult of the ego.

MAURICE BARRÈS, 1897

One of the main driving forces of fascism was nationalism. Italian fascism grew out of the interventionism of the First World War, and National Socialism grew out of the nationalism of German Austria and the Germans in Bohemia. However, a strange feature of this phenomenon was that, though this nationalism almost always started off by being strictly concerned with its own people, it soon assumed a kind of missionary universalism, and

Franz Seldte who founded the *Stahlhelm*, the right-wing ex-serviceman's organization in 1918. He participated in the *Harzburger Front* in October 1931 in which the Nazi party and the German National People's Party decided to boycott the parliamentary rule of the Weimar Republic.

thus the characteristics of imperialism. Although the luck of the German army had totally run out by July 1918 and it suffered its first decisive defeat on 8 August, the nationalists continued to believe that it was 'unbeaten in the field'. In fascist Italy Vittorio Veneto was re-styled the decisive battle of the First World War. Every school book described how Italy 'had determined the course of the whole war at the glorious battle of Vittorio Veneto'. Mussolini believed that Italian imperialism would succeed that of the Prussians and the British. He wanted to solve all Italy's economic problems, not by internal political remedies, but through expansion, by colonizing North Africa. But that meant war and conquests, the 'imperialism of the poor' against the rich nations. Mussolini borrowed, from pre-war Italian nationalism, the concept of the totality of the nation, a totality which embraces all classes and eliminates all class conflicts; the same principle applied to the National Socialist concept of *Volksgemeinschaft*. In the case of Mussolini, as also in the rest of European fascism, there was the idea of the unification of nationalism and socialism. He had proclaimed the slogan 'war or republic' as early as 1915. Even before the war he had written that the organized workers could not deny their own nationality. The influence of Sorel's thought on the young Mussolini is unmistakable.

Beginning with interventionist nationalism, Mussolini maintained his belief in the overriding importance of foreign policy right up until 1940, in order to give fascism one more task to fulfil after it had overcome communism, and in order to spare it 'the miserable fate of the *Rinnovamento*'. At the latest after the failure of the 'grain battle', the *Battaglio del Grano*, Italy went over to an expansionist policy of settlement. As Mussolini had always had a very strict view of socialism it was not hard for him to find similar stern virtues in nationalism. Life and war became the civic duty of each individual, culminating in the war of conquest, the *conquista*. The doctrine of fascism did state that the *Impero* was not merely a territorial, military or economic concept, but also had spiritual and moral implications, in the sense of a hegemony which was not based merely on territory. But that was more the result of attempts to give a spiritual disguise to the will to revive the ancient Roman Empire, and also to the essentially warlike philosophy of fascism, which Mussolini had proclaimed as early as September 1922.

Almost every European fascism had similar nationalistic, military and imperialistic tendencies. The Russian fascists wanted Russia to become the leading power in Europe and Asia and its territory to include Finland, Latvia, Lithuania, Esthonia, Poland, Galicia, Rumania, Bulgaria, Persia, Afghanistan and Mongolia. They laid claim to Finland, while the Finnish fascists envisaged the eastern frontiers of their Great Finland as stretching as far as the Urals. The Arrow Cross of the Hungarian

Metropolitan State University
Library Services

fascists was intended to call to mind the mythical empire of the Scythians in the Danube area; similarly the Czech nationalists dreamed of reviving the Great Moravian Empire of early medieval times. As for the Rumanian fascists, they believed in the words of the poet, Eugène Ionescu, 'Le Roumain est un animal nationaliste.' Because Rumania had already experienced a long colonial period she had a certain feeling of inferiority and cut herself off from all her neighbours. Similar imperialist tendencies can be observed in Spanish and Portuguese nationalism and fascism. As with all the fascisms they were concerned with two things – first, the conquest of the state, and then, once they had secured power in their own country, foreign conquest. In the 1920s the Norwegian Peasants' Party, which in a sense was the germ cell of Norwegian fascism, had a very radical foreign policy and regarded the claim to Greenland as an expression of a *mare nostrum* idea.

But these nationalist elements within fascism were also the cause of fundamental differences. European fascism could only achieve a temporary unity through the hegemony of the two fascist powers during the war. Their nationalism carried within it the seeds of deep conflict. This was shown by the impossibility of achieving a compromise between the demands for a Great Netherlands and for a Great Flanders, and by the national rivalries between the peoples of the Balkans. Indeed, nationalism played a decisive role in the development of fascism in the Balkans after 1918. Long before 1914 there had been a latent spirit of aggressive nationalism in that area. After 1918 it had to be channelled into establishing internal unity as all possibilities of irredentism were blocked by the big powers. The same applied to Slovakia and Croatia until the Second World War seemed to offer, briefly, the possibility for their dreams of an empire to be realized.

However important nationalism was for all the European fascisms, it must be borne in mind that it was still only one of the driving forces. Alone it would never have led to fascism – at most it might have led to a traditionalist kind of integral national-

Members of the
Croix de Feu leaving
the Church of St
Nicholas after a
memorial service
honouring their dead
comrades, killed
during the Paris riots
of February 1934.

ism, like that of the *Action Française* or the *Deutsch-nationale Volkspartei* in the Weimar Republic. However, the nationalism of the fascists was not restricted merely to the nation state, but was imperialistic. The two leading European fascisms, Italian and German fascism, were at the same time revolutionary and 'subversive' (Salvatorelli), and extremely reactionary – far more so than the national conservatives, who merely wanted to go back to the national state of the nineteenth century, to the *Risorgimento* and to Bismarck's Reich. But the fascists looked to the universal imperialism of the *Imperium Romanum* or the Holy Roman Empire. Hitler and Mussolini were forced to abandon certain essential points in their programmes and ideologies in their urge for expansion, for an imperialist foreign policy. We have already seen something of this in the development of the *Waffen-SS*.

The *völkisch* policy of conquest that Hitler had developed by February 1926, and the concept of world domination outlined by Himmler several times after 1940, were indeed quite logical in themselves. What they failed to recognize was that these ideas could not be implemented with the time and human and technical means at their disposal. The 'territorial policy of the future' which Hitler proclaimed in 1926, led to his fundamental rejection of the traditional kind of *völkisch* nationalism. Himmler too, who saw himself as the *Saatzüchter der Nation* (seed-grower of the nation), commented in September 1940 that if good Germanic blood did not multiply, 'we will not be able to rule the earth'. Here nationalism of the traditional European kind was thrown overboard for the sake of imperialist aims. Neither Italy nor the other European fascisms would or could go along with this.

Militarism

In 1925 Arturo Labriola called fascism a phenomenon of 'spontaneous militarism'. Indeed, for every fascist movement the army of its own country was politically taboo. The ideologization of war and their foreign policies brought them on to the side of the army from the very beginning. In Germany, as in Italy, disappointment over the outcome of the First World War led to an exaggerated mythologization of war as a necessary phenomenon of human life. Of course, the preponderant position of the army within the state and in society was not a fascist invention. In fact, the fascists considerably limited the political influence of the army, creating instead the concept of the 'political soldier' of the fascist party, which was inevitably regarded by the army as an internal political opponent. An example of this was the conflict between the army and the SA under Röhm which led to his murder in June 1934, and the exclusion of the SA from Germany's political life, thus allowing the rise of the SS, which was to become a far more dangerous opponent of the army. In the fascist regimes the fighting forces, like the whole nation, were used primarily as a means with which to achieve hidden political aims.

The First World War was doubtless the greatest single cause of the rise of fascism. The millions of disappointed soldiers returning home to an economy which could not assimilate them provided the breeding ground for fascism. Those who took part in the first meeting of the *fasci di combattimento* in Milan in March 1919 were all ex-soldiers. They, the *arditi di guerra*, formed the core of the fascist movement which then developed. The case was similar in Germany with the National Socialist movement, and for the other European fascisms. One must also bear in mind that many of them were young and were still being trained when the war ended, so that they had not yet had experience at the front. Heinrich Himmler and Ernst von Salomon were two examples of extreme German nationalists in the Weimar Republic who had not been at the front, but perhaps for that very reason had very radical political views. It is interesting that in 1928 Giuseppe Bottai, Under-Secretary of State in the Ministry of Corporations and a fascist 'of the first hour', criticized the socialists for not accepting that these ex-soldiers who had returned from the war represented 'a new moral aristocracy, a new national force'. But in 1922 the socialist Giovanni Zibordi explained in his study, *Critica sozialista del fascismo*, that fascism not only represented the conscious response of the bourgeoisie and the resentment of the lower middle classes, but also 'the violent revolution of *déclassé* soldiers' in the face of the unreal, though terrifying threat of a socialist revolution in a country already deeply stricken by the war.

The belief that the 'aristocracy of the trenches' was crucial to all the European fascist movements becomes more meaningful when one bears in mind that economic difficulties encouraged the creation of a new warrior elite. Just as during the war the Italian volunteers were exposed to the taunts of their socialist comrades, so the young German nationalists who flocked to the *Freikorps* of the Social Democratic government, were regarded with utter hatred by the socialist masses. An example of this is given by Ernst von Salomon in his novel *Die Geächteten* (The Despised) (1930), where he describes the Kapp putsch. The young nationalist volunteers were confronted by the deadly hostility of the workers. 'A wave of dull hatred wafted up to us from the crowd – the hatred of two races, full of disgust for each other.'

It can of course be said that these opposing forces did meet, as is often maintained of socialism and nationalism. But basically this amalgamation has never succeeded. Either socialism or nationalism falls by the wayside. Only for the purpose of political propaganda was this symbiosis, this 'syndrome', so useful.

The experience of the front was of crucial importance for many fascist, or pre-fascist leaders. Engelbert Dollfuss, who as a young man volunteered and after many difficulties managed to join the *Kaiserjäger* (Imperial Rifles), never forgot his experiences. After the defeat in 1918 he left the army, but declared that 'our policies must not be allowed to go astray – we men of the front must see to it. The main thing is that we must keep alive our spirit of comradeship, a true comradeship, all through our lives.' It is not necessary to emphasize again the importance that Hitler's experience of the army in the war, the first serious commitment of his life, had for his later development. For the French fascists too, in addition to the monarchistic traditionalism of the *Action Française*, the spirit of the *Unions de combattants*, the associations formed by men who had fought at the front, was of great importance. Mosley's political views were formed during his war service and his work in the war economy after 1916. They could all, like Mussolini, claim to 'have had a taste of the trenches'.

Nor should one forget the importance for the fascists of symbol and ritual. Flags, standards, military songs and parades, uniforms with military

insignia, daggers, death's-head flags over their
writing desks, steel helmets and leather flying jackets,
marches and para-military organizations, – all are
proof of fascism's eminently military characteristics.
It is significant that Mussolini, who in 1919 had
claimed that he could carry the whole of Italy with
him, always looked back with nostalgia to his life
as a soldier, when he was given firm commands to
obey. 'That was the life. I shall abdicate, I shall
abdicate. For who is going to give me orders now!'

This leads us to an essential phenomenon of all
the fascist movements – the building up of militant
private armies which were the first step towards the
outbreak of civil war. They formed the hard core
of the mass movement. Their primary purpose was
terrorism. Alff rightly points out that the acts of
terrorism practised by the *arditi* and the SA were
by no means repugnant to the rank and file of the
party. On the contrary, it could be said that these
acts of violence attracted them. An important factor

The fascist youth
organization,
Balillas, parades in
celebration of its
second anniversary in
front of the *Palazzo
Venezia* in Rome.

is that within the parliamentary democracies independent party power machines were being formed
which were directed as much against the state itself
as against its own political enemies within the state.
In 1931, in the French edition of his work, *La
technique du coup d'état*, Curzio Malaparte pointed
out that Mussolini had never intended to appear as
the saviour of the state, but had been solely concerned
with taking it over. 'This programme was far more
honest than the one he produced in 1919.' He
commented that fascism, despite the fact that it was
an anti-party, took on the appearance of a proper
parliamentary party until it had built up a militant,
armed organization. Only then could it reveal its
true nature.

It should be borne in mind, however, that the
fascists were by no means the first to set up militant
fighting organizations. Alff maintains that in the
case of Austria, private fascist armies like the
Heimwehr did not develop in reaction to violence
from the left. But that is not correct. By the middle
of December 1918 serious conflicts had broken out
between the Social Democrat workers of Floridsdorf
and the Red Guard during their attempted *coups*.
At all events it can be said that the development of
radical right- and left-wing para-military organizations was virtually simultaneous. When the Austrian
Republic began to fail, the conflict between the Social
Democrat *Schutzbund* and the extreme right-wing
Heimwehr was intensified, and their internal struggles
fatally weakened the state long before Hitler finally
destroyed it.

The close relationship between fascism and war
must be remembered. War was fascism's 'true
element'. The entire structure of the state and its
policies were geared to war. To this extent fascism
was a permanent state of emergency. The fascists
constantly emphasized that the nation was in a state
of crisis and that this must inevitably lead to military
action.

Both Hitler and Mussolini gave reasons for their
militaristic attitude from the beginning. When
Mussolini served with the *Bersaglieri* in Verona,

BERLIN, VI. JAHRGANG   3. (VERSTÄRKTE) FOLGE, 1939

Der Schulungsbrief

Wehr-
Wille und Kraft

Herausgeber: Der Reichsorganisationsleiter der NSDAP.

Title page of a Nazi periodical, specifically designed to indoctrinate the armed forces.

he wrote to his captain after the death of his mother that it was good to remember the heroes who had shed their blood for the unity of the fatherland. But it was even better to be active, to help create a strong bulwark of human bodies to hold back any attempt by the 'northern barbarians' to reduce Italy to a mere geographical expression. When he wrote for his local paper in 1908 a study of the philosophy of violence, revealing how strongly he was influenced by Nietzsche, he celebrated these new 'free spirits', strengthened by the war, by their experience of loneliness and great danger. Mussolini saw socialism too, as did his teacher Sorel, primarily as a battle, as a war which 'is almost always the prelude to revolution'. From the beginning he was at one with the European socialists who in August were in favour of the war against the Central Powers, 'against Prussian and Pan-German militarism'.

Hitler, who had never gone through a socialist phase, was from the very beginning a German nationalist. Thus for both of them, the outbreak of the First World War in 1914 fulfilled their secret longings. At the same time it can be said that the militant nationalism which was inherent in the 'ideas of 1914' was one of the sources of European fascism.

The private, para-military armies of the fascist leaders were never used against the armies of their own countries and they carefully avoided coming into conflict with them. Often the army in fact formed the ideological and concrete basis of the country's fascist movement, as was the case with the Hungarian Arrow Cross party, which envisaged the army as the binding force of the Danubian-Carpathian Great Fatherland. So too Mussolini proclaimed before the march on Rome that the cause of fascism was the cause of the army, for during the preceding years the army had put its weapons at the disposal of the fascists. Although the National Socialists did violently condemn the commanders of the *Reichswehr* in their publications, they never attacked the army itself. After 1933 Hitler used this army against his private army, the SA, to build up the Third Reich.

The influence of the army was always strong in semi-fascist military dictatorships like Poland's *militocracie* during and after the period of Pilsudski's rule. Then the army was an iron clamp which held the country together. But it was a real enthusiasm for the military on the part of the population which enabled the army to act this part. This brought the fascists the sympathy of many high-ranking professional officers in almost all European countries. Fuller is but one example. This attitude developed as a result of the indifference shown towards the military in the parliamentary democracies. A soldier could expect more from fascism.

Many historians who have studied fascism doubt whether either racialism or anti-Semitism was necessarily a pre-condition or consequence of fascism. There certainly were fascist movements which had nothing to do with the racialist theories that in some cases led to genocide. For example, Mosley did not emphasize anti-Semitism until several years after his movement's foundation, when it began to look for inspiration to the German Nazi rather than the Italian fascist model. The more the British fascists identified with the Nazis, the more racialist and anti-Semitic they became. When Turati claimed in 1928 that fascism was possible anywhere in Europe – a thesis which was by no means generally accepted – he justified this claim by pointing out that the world existed in a permanent state of war. Therefore, he maintained, in modern society distinctions are made according to race and not class – one tiny master race confronting a vast race of slaves.

The causes and motives of this racialism had a dual nature. On the one hand the fascists attempted to escape from the drab present to the far-off world of antiquity which they mythologized and idealized. The Romans, the *Germanen*, the Celts, the Scythians and the ancient Finno-Ugrian tribes were all in turn exploited to give historical foundations to their ideology of a *völkisch* community of the future. Thus they transferred the socialist concept of the class struggle on to an international level of political conflict – between the rich and the poor nations. Hitler attempted to confront the British ideology of the chosen people with London as the eternal Jerusalem, with his *Weltanschauung* of the Aryans and *Germanen* as the 'race soul' of the chosen Aryan and Germanic nations.

The French fascists endeavoured to trace their past back to Celtic France. But basically these traditions – the Celts, the Gothic spires, Renaissance literature around Rabelais – were beyond the pale of France's 'classical' history. Even today Frenchmen refer to a stupid and rude joke as a *gauloiserie*. Léon Degrelle referred to himself as a *Germane* and believed that the greatest period of his

Racialism

Reich minister, Alfred Rosenberg, whose *Myth of the 20th Century* made a lasting influence on Hitler. Although one of the main Nazi ideologists his influence and power declined after Hitler's accession.

country was when it was called *Germania inferior*. In the Balkans racialism and anti-Semitism were the main motives behind fascism. They had roots going back to the nineteenth century, and derived from a wide-spread xenophobia which was also directed against powerful national minorities, such as the industrial workers in Rumania, many of whom were originally Hungarian, or the Transylvanian Saxons, and the Austrians, Germans, Czechs and Slovaks in Hungary. Social problems which existed between the peoples were deliberately made into national and racial problems with the

purpose of establishing *l'union nationaliste raciste.*
For all these fascisms it was really a matter solely
of racial, national egoism.

As race became more important than *Volk* and
state, a race of alien stock was inevitably seen as the
enemy which had to be fought, even to the point of
annihilation. The logic of this was to apply the ideas
of social Darwinism to their own society and produce
the concept of the *Unterrasse*, an inferior race
whose members were then declared to be *Untermenschen* – sub-human and asocial – to be exterminated by work in the concentration camps.

Interestingly, almost all the fascist leaders failed
to come up to the racial standards they had themselves set up. An obvious case is that of the National
Socialist leaders. In Italy, where racialism had
been merely taken over from the Germans, it was
less marked. This phenomenon was noticeable
wherever there were strong feelings of racialism, as
in the Balkans. Julius Gömbös, the Hungarian
Prime Minister from 1932 to 1936, came from a
Transylvanian German family called Knöpfle. In
such cases it was a matter of artificial assimilation,
which may have been quite genuine in the case of an
individual, but which was difficult to reconcile with
the principles of their *Weltanschauung.*

The moral abyss into which this nationalist
racialism led was shown by the fact that they no
longer confined themselves to denying their opponents any human qualities, but denied them even
their biological existence.

The weeding out had to be done for reasons of
state so that the flower-beds could flourish. This
work of 'cultivation' included the 'pacification' of
whole cities such as Warsaw and Leningrad – i.e.
razing them to the ground. Himmler regarded the
Slavs as having the souls of slaves – it was no more
possible to have relations with them than it was for
the Germans to have relations with negroes. The
master race must be absolutely separate from the
alien, working races (who were to be cut off from
any cultural development) if it was to avoid the fate
of Greece and Rome. In fact it was a world based

Reinhard Heydrich, who after Himmler was second in command of the SS and the Gestapo.

on murder and suppression disguised with ideological trimmings, as Ernst Jünger prophesied in his novel *On the Marble Cliffs*, which was published in 1939 shortly before the outbreak of the Second World War. This modern, inhuman barbarism culminated in 1941 with the war of conquest, ideology and settlement in the USSR that Hitler had demanded as early as 1926. 'We will call a halt to the eternal movement of the *Germanen* to the south and west of Europe, and we will look to the lands in the east.' This was no longer a question of eastern or western orientation, but was now a matter of '*Ostpolitik*, meaning the acquisition of enough land to satisfy the needs of the German people'. In February 1933 he had addressed the army commanders on the subject of the ruthless Germanization of the east. The Slav peoples, if they could not be made German, were to be treated as animals which could be destroyed without any moral scruples.

Although German fascism was unique in its fanaticism and brutality, racialism undoubtedly played a part in all the European fascist movements. They all, even the Italians, claimed that they wanted to create a new kind of citizen, who would be totally loyal to the people, the state and the party, the *homo fascistus*. Mussolini dreamed of manufacturing a new race in the laboratory of Italy. Again and again he spoke of the blood that turned the wheels of history. When he failed to weld his Italians into a single people of Romans, he blamed it on the four million slaves 'that Rome carried in her bosom, to her misfortune'. Then, finally, he took over Hitler's racial theories and established a system of general inspection '*della razza*' in the Republic of Salò. But this was as a result of German pressure, and Mussolini reverted to his spiritual origins, secretly condemning Pan-German militarism, as he had done before 1914 and during the First World War.

Neo-heathen tendencies which were cultivated in Hitler's Germany, above all by the SS, failed to take hold in Mussolini's Italy, despite various utterances by the Duce. Although he liked to talk of the old Roman or Italian race which had been resurrected by the war and by his political activity, a race 'which carries within it the treasure of eternal youth', he cared far too much about the state to subordinate his heterogeneous empire to any racial concept. *Razzismo* only began to acquire significance shortly before the war; in July 1938 the *Manifesto della Razza* was proclaimed. More and more Jews lost their jobs as civil servants, but there were no attempts to destroy them economically, morally or physically, as in Germany. Julius Evola, who had spoken of 'unworthy life' in 1928, regarded race as having above all a spiritual value which could not be nullified by miscegenation. He called on Germany to 'break down the barriers created by racial fanaticism and racial nationalism'. The purely biological, vulgar-Darwinist attitude to race was alien to Italian fascism. Many of the European fascist movements used the concept of race in this vague sense. Vidkun Quisling in Norway spoke of the superiority of the Nordic and Germanic race that lived around the North Sea, although like Hamsun he did not include the English, whom he regarded as racially contaminated by the Jews.

Once it is made clear that racialism was an essential factor in fascism, it follows that anti-Semitism was its pre-condition or consequence. In 1939, in his study *Die Juden und Europa*, Max Horkheimer rightly pointed out that 'whole armies of unemployed and the lower middle classes love Hitler above all else because of his anti-Semitism, and the core of the ruling class share this love.' The anti-Semitism of the twentieth century is different in kind from that of earlier centuries, even though both have led to the slaughter of Jews. Medieval anti-Semitism was a religious phenomenon: baptized Jews were safe from persecution and could be accepted into the community. But modern anti-Semitism is based on the pseudo-scientific racial 'laws' of nineteenth-century writers such as Gobineau: the Jew is marked out for life, and is given no chance to escape his fate.

Arthur Schnitzler's novels written before 1914 show the explosive quality of anti-Semitism in Austria, and particularly in Vienna, at that time. As a schoolboy Hitler had been brought up as an anti-Semite by his Pan-German teachers in Linz. It is significant that in Vienna, despite his admiration for the political ideas of von Schönerer and Karl Lueger, he did not join their parties. The only organization he became a member of was the *Antisemitenbund* (League of anti-Semites). In Vienna he had ample opportunity to observe the strong influence of the Jews in art, literature and the press, but what he deliberately chose to ignore was that these Jews were essentially anti-Slav and orientated towards Germany. After 1918, under the influence of the Russian *émigrés*, it became easy for him to identify the bolsheviks with the Jews. Even at that time he expressed his regret that the 'Hebrews', whom he regarded not as a religious community but as a race, had not been held under poisonous gas, and advocated their 'elimination'. He gradually came to regard them as the 'counter-race'.

After the prelude provided by the occupation of Poland in 1939, Hitler was able to give vent to his infernal hatred in Russia from 1941 onwards. For him the Jews and the Russian leaders were identical; the Russian people consisted of *Untermenschen* – sub-humans – and the 'eternal Jews' were 'beasts in human form' which had to be exterminated. 'They will be killed like flies', according to the pamphlet *Der Untermensch* which Himmler published in Germany in an edition of nearly four million, and which was published in fourteen other languages. For him the Russians were animals ruled by commissars: both they and the Jews had to be weeded out and destroyed. In 1938 the top Nazi party judge, Walter Buch, proclaimed that: 'The Jew is not a human being, but merely a symptom of rot.' As Hitler despised the Jews and the Russians equally, he had no intention of allowing a new Russia, purified of Jews and bolsheviks, to rise again as a national entity, particularly as he wanted the territory. This explains Hitler's total indifference to and rejection of General Vlasov's collaborationist Russian movement.

In contrast, Italian anti-Semitism, like its racialism, was merely a façade assumed in order to please the Germans. There were, of course, some small anti-Semitic groups, such as that of Giovanni Preziosi. But Mussolini's anti-Semitic race laws of 1938 were not even taken seriously by the party secretary, Roberto Farinacci. Only after 1943, during the Republic of Salò, did the deportations to the east start to take place. The new party programme of Verona published in 1943, stated that: 'Members of the Jewish race are foreigners. During this war they are to be treated as members of a foreign nation.' But by that time fascism was already practically dead.

By 1940 the fascist historian Gioacchino Volpe had pointed out that racialism and anti-Semitism in the Anglo-Saxon and German sense had never existed in Italy, despite the laws of 1938. However, he admitted that at any time it was possible for any of the fascist anti-movements to turn into anti-Semitism. Volpe hinted too that it was merely on account of Germany that Mussolini was going along with anti-Semitism, and he admitted that it was meeting with hostility and resistance amongst the people. It was mainly the disapproval of the Pope and the Catholic Church that reinforced Mussolini's anti-Semitic attitude. Several laws were passed banning Jews from teaching and scientific posts, but even then there was no intention of persecuting the Jews as in Germany.

In the Balkans after 1918 anti-Semitism took on a totally different character. Here it became the strongest motive behind the spirit of nationalism. In these predominantly agrarian countries it was mainly the Jewish section of the population, together with other minority groups, that determined intellectual and economic development. In this part of Europe therefore, anti-Semitism had a long history; it also had roots in central Europe, but often for different reasons. In the countries of the Balkans and east central Europe, the young intelligentsia, in search of the essence of their nation, turned to the peasantry. In this almost exclusively agrarian society, therefore, the civilized, urban, Jewish population was automatically rejected as representing an alien culture. This hostile rejection was matched by an equally strong anti-communism. In line with Russian tradition, the Russian fascist *émigrés* tended to stand for an extreme anti-Semitism. Also the 'White terror' practised by the Hungarian nationalists in 1919 was directed almost exclusively against the Jews. The fact that Béla Kun, the leader of the Hungarian Soviet Republic, was a Jew, suited them perfectly. Christianity and anti-Semitism conditioned each other, although the later was alien to the bulk of the Magyar people. In the division of labour which developed naturally in Hungary, the

German tended to be a carpenter, the Slovak a glazier, the Hungarian a peasant and the Jew a tradesman. Thus anti-Semitism was a minority attitude.

It must not be forgotten, however, that there were some fascist movements which did not put a decisive emphasis on anti-Semitism. At first neither Mosley in Britain, nor Mussert in the Netherlands, was openly anti-Semitic, though eventually their propaganda acquired an anti-Semitic flavour in response partly to Jewish denunciations. Their nations were no more anti-Semitic than the Danes and Norwegians. Mussert distinguished between three Jewish groups – those who were nationalists, whom he accepted into his party; the Zionists whom he tolerated as foreign guests; and the so-called international Marxist-bolshevik Jews. Quisling came to anti-Semitism via his strongly Christian faith. Bucard's *Francisme*, like Italian fascism, rejected anti-Semitism. Gustave Hervé's *Milice Socialiste National* rejected freemasons, but not the Jews. Pilsudski was even attacked by the Polish Nationalist Party for being philo-Semitic. It was only his successors who wanted to achieve racial purity and to get rid of the Jews, not by destroying them but by encouraging emigration to Palestine. The shock troops of the National Party confined themselves to smashing the windows of Jewish shops.

It was mainly Hitler's National Socialists who were prepared to carry their anti-Semitism through to the final extreme. They sought to justify their action 'scientifically' by adopting the ideas of social Darwinism. Processes which were purely biological were made absolute and transferred onto a political and social plane. They regarded Darwin's process of 'natural selection' as the pre-condition of all human development. Hitler believed in one divine commandment – that of preserving the species. But the state that had the most racially valuable people had the right to expand at the cost of other peoples and to destroy the 'lower' races. Within Germany these were the Jews, the gipsies, Jehovah's Witnesses and other groups which failed to meet the approval of the National Socialists. Abroad they were, according to circumstances, the 'Jew-ridden' English, French, neutrals, the defeated Czechs, Poles and Russians and finally the entire population of the earth, where it was not fascist. Hitler's hatred of the Jews was the determining factor behind all his political actions. From the very beginning his aim had been to destroy what he saw as this 'counter-race'. The scurrilous idea of confining them in a 'ghetto for wild animals' was a mere temporary measure. His ultimate aim was always total exter-mination. He was determined to avenge Germany's defeat in 1918, which he regarded as a Jewish plot. On 30 January 1939 Hitler proclaimed that if the international financiers were determined to provoke a Second World War, it would end, not with the bolshevization of the world, but with the 'extermination of the Jewish race in Europe'. This extermination began with the Jewish reservations after the Polish campaign in 1939, and reached its culmination in the extermination camps in eastern Europe after 1941.

The reign of terror

Such are the dungeons above which the castles of the tyrant are built . . . grim, stinking caves which provide entertainment for those creatures whose depravity has damned them for all eternity, who rejoice in the desecration of all human dignity and freedom.
ERNST JÜNGER, Summer 1939

Sir Oswald Mosley wrote in his memoirs that fascism was evoked by people who wanted to achieve a national rebirth. But they were also people who saw themselves confronted by an abyss of decadence and death. Here he put his finger on one of the pri-mary motives behind the growth of fascism – the terror which leads people to strike out in wild violence at anything around them which appears to be an opponent. Thus, as Alff has formulated it, the suppressed turned into the suppressors, the tortured became the torturers. George L. Mosse's view that mass terror and mass extermination were not the characteristic of European fascism is only partly correct, for an eagerness to adopt a tactic of violence cannot be ignored in European fascism. National Socialism was merely the extreme manifestation of this tendency.

The modern political mass movements, such as fascism, but also communism and other forms of substitute for the old Churches, are not solely based on the alienation of man in modern industrial society, but to an equally great extent on the loss of the former ties which helped to give meaning to people's lives. Now the middle classes, fearing the bolshevist threat to their privileged position, turned to the prophets of the nineteenth century whom they had previously mocked. 'For fascism, as an effective movement, was born of fear.' But it must be added that behind this very material fear there was a fundamental *Lebensangst*, a spiritual fear; the myth of violence was also a substitute for values which people could no longer believe in, and a defence against an opponent with very concrete ideas about the rebuilding of society which would mean the abdication of the middle class, their own class.

Thus it came to the glorification of terror and violence, which sprang from dark impulses in the uneducated masses as well as among romantic intellectuals. Even a man like Himmler, despite his mystic worship of Hitler as a kind of radiant demi-god, as the saviour of *Germanentum* from the onslaught of the bolshevik peril from the east, never quite lost this vague sense of fear.

Here, too, death symbolism played an important part in the fascist movements. All European nationalist movements paid tribute to this death cult, whether they were conservative or fascist, traditionalist or revolutionary. For Maurice Barrès the death cult guaranteed the continued existence of 'France éternelle'. The fascists as well as the National Socialists emphasized the symbolic significance of their heroes in celebrating the deaths of those who had fallen before the seizure of power. This link with death was particularly pronounced in the Rumanian Iron Guard. They sought to become one with the spirit of the people in a kind of holy ecstasy. The 'nest', the smallest unit in the movement, became a 'death team'.

Whoever worships death and the dead in this way can be no stranger to violence. Thus it can be rightly pointed out that National Socialism did not live according to the model of Italian fascism, but according to 'the seductive success of their use of violence'. Violence and the use of violence were the elements of life for Mussolini – from the beginning until the end when he died by violence. As early as 1908, as a student of Sorel and Pareto, he had written a study entitled 'The Philosophy of Violence' for the Republican newspaper of his native province. It must be borne in mind too that the Italian syndicalists, as well as the nationalists, were followers of Sorel. That was why fascism, after being amalgamated with the Nationalists, acquired its dual nature, being both conservative and revolutionary. It never managed to master this inner conflict. We have already pointed out what little store the fascist leaders put on their programmes: they were concerned with action, pure and simple. The *Doctrine of Fascism* declared that the state not only embodied ethical content, authority and power, but was also an organization which needed to expand. Mussolini simply applied his own feeling about life to the state, in the form of the 'doctrine of action'. Basing his ideas on Nietzsche and Stirner, the Duce proclaimed his belief in a 'philosophy of violence' which dominated the whole fascist philosophy of the function of the state. Instead of discussion, in the manner of the liberal and democratic systems, there was to be 'the methodical use of violence'.

It would be a mistake to equate the use of terror in fascist Italy with that used in Nazi Germany and in the Soviet Union under Stalin. During the twenty years of the Italian fascist regime 21,000 people came before the special court for the defence of the state. There were never more than about 5,000 in

The memorial to those killed in the fighting following the abortive Munich 'beer cellar' putsch of November, 1923.

protective custody or banished to punishment islands, but for those who were victims it was hard enough as Ignazio Silone and Cesare Pavese testify in their novel, *The Comrade*. From the beginning, fascism was deliberately and unscrupulously dedicated to violence. The *squadristi* and the brown-shirts of the NSDAP formed what Tasca aptly described as the 'fascism of extermination' and the 'counter-revolution by blood'. It all depended on which side of the grave one stood. In 1928 Giuseppe Bottai described this use of violence as 'a disciplined and ordered act of retribution'. In 1926 Margherita G. Sarfatti, Mussolini's intellectual friend, even compared the notorious punitive expeditions made by the fascists against the headquarters of the socialists and the unions with those burlesque jokes 'which in earlier times Italians had laughed at in the puppet theatre of Pulcinello and Arlechino'. That was a most distasteful understatement, to be sure, but if one compares the acts of violence committed by the Italian fascists with those of the Nazis in Germany, one is almost inclined to agree with her.

When M. J. Bonn undertook his comparative analysis of the various fascist movements in 1928 in his collected volume *Internationaler Faschismus*, he was already convinced that they were not identical because of their particular national features. 'Perhaps the only thing they all have in common is their belief in physical violence as the basic means of forming and governing the community.' By 1919, as a young student, Codreanu was learning about the use of violence, about street fighting, discipline and action in the small, radical, nationalist groups around the anti-Semite Cuza. Political murders were planned and carried out. The political fanaticism of the Iron Guard with its 'death groups', which were always ready to kill or be killed, was more extreme than in any other fascist movement in Europe, although they all made use of violence.

The Russian fascists after 1918 regarded themselves as the protectors of the good, and were prepared to use brutality in dealing with any opposition. They saw their opponent as a diabolical power which 'gathered all that was evil in the dregs of humanity' into military cadres – and which used these bands of robbers to terrorize the peaceful, working population. The violence inherent in the anti-Republican ideology of Charles Maurras in France has already been mentioned. The *Camelots du Roi*, the *Action Française*'s volunteer corps, were the pioneers of the organized street fighting units that in the next century were to terrorize fascism's political opponents. However, when they were first founded their tactics were confined to relatively peaceful matters such as propaganda and street selling.

Jose Antonio Primo de Rivera taught his Falange

the significance of violence. Where justice and the fatherland were concerned, they need use no other arguments than their fists and pistols. The stewards whom Mosley organized to protect his meetings from his political opponents and who acted with extreme brutality, were compared to the German SA. The far more radical and extreme anti-Semitic Imperial Fascist League of Arnold Spencer suggested the use of death chambers for the 'solution' of the Jewish problem in 1935.

If these were merely figments of perverted political imaginations, in Germany terrorist radicals were given the opportunity of realizing these fantasies. By February 1920, when Hitler proclaimed the new programme of the re-named *National-sozialistische Deutsche Arbeiterpartei*, he emphasized the importance of the fighting that took place in meetings and in the streets. As Hitler expressed it, the party was now replacing a weak and cowardly defence with a courageous and brutal attack. Although by 1939 the system of political terror was virtually complete, Hitler still found the various precautions which were necessary on account of his aims in foreign affairs extremely irritating. Above all, he hated the lawyers and the intellectuals. He would have liked, as he declared to the press on 10 November 1938, to have 'exterminated them or something'. But the Nazis realized that they could put such ideas into practice only after achieving military victories, after which they also believed that they would be able to do without the Churches.

First of all, the war gave them the opportunity of practising terrorism on the peoples they had conquered. Goebbels proclaimed triumphantly in April 1940 that National Socialism would now carry out in Europe the revolution it had accomplished in Germany, where its political opponents had not realized what was happening up until 1932. This was due to the party's tactical ruse of assuming a legal disguise. The German slogan now was *Lebensraum*. 'That can be interpreted according to will.' This eventually included the idea of the 'special treatment' of entire peoples and racial and

A placard of the Spanish Falange with the slogan 'Spain awake, Spain forwards'.

military groups, such as the Russian commissars, leading via the idea of 'pacification', which meant the annihilation of entire cities, to the system of concentration camps during the war, which were a mixture of terror and forced labour. This terrorization was carried out with total disregard for any system of norms, for Hitler never committed himself again according to the Nuremberg laws. The instrument he used for this system of 'extermination through work' was Himmler's SS.

As the war grew worse for the Germans, demanding an unexpected amount of human resources, the Nazi leaders were gradually forced, not to think, but to act differently. They put an end to their mass executions of Russian prisoners of war. Moslems who had up till then been executed because they were circumcized were now found to have many of the qualities which would enable them to become members of the SS. In the last months of the war the concentration camps in the Reich had about 60,000 prisoners working in underground factories in Thuringia and the Harz. In January 1945 there were 714,211 prisoners in concentration camps, guarded by 40,000 SS men. These few figures are enough to show that in terms of amount and intensity in the use of violence and terror, the National Socialist regime was far ahead of all the fascist regimes. Only the fascist regimes in Rumania and Croatia were comparable, not in terms of the extent of their power, but in the extremism of their ideas and practices.

As the war gradually brought about the collapse of the fascist powers their terrorization of their own peoples grew more brutal. In the fascist Republic of Salò, and in Hitler's Reich, the leaders finally wished for the destruction even of their own people, for they had failed to come up to their expectations. Ultimately all they were left with was the urge for total destruction.

*Every kind of fascism (white,
red and black) mastered only
too well the technique of
brutalizing human beings.*
ANGELO TASCA

The totalitarian element

Although it was Mussolini who coined the term
'totalitarian' to describe his fascist regime, many
historians do not consider that fascism in Italy ever
developed into a modern dictatorship. It was in no
way comparable with the totalitarian regimes in
Germany and the Soviet Union. Carl J. Friedrich
has defined four decisive and two secondary elements
of a totalitarian system of rule. The former were the
existence of a unity party, an official ideology
comprising a kind of 'political Messianism', a
total monopoly of the press media and a terrorist
secret police. The secondary elements were the
monopoly of weapons and the controlled economy.
The fact that, despite Mussolini's declarations to
the contrary, ideology had very little importance
in fascist Italy, has already been mentioned. When
necessary, the convinced fascists 'of the first hour'
made do, for purposes of intellectual export, with
Gentile's concept of the 'ethical state'.

An important factor in how fascists saw themselves
was their belief in 'totalitarianism', even though, up
until the end, various powerful forces continued to
exist outside the framework of the system, like the
monarchy, the army and the Church. In fact, these
forces contributed considerably to the overthrow of
fascism. At the party congress of June 1925, Mussolini
had proclaimed the *Volontà totalitaria* to be the
highest law. Mussolini's ultimate aim was to establish
the *stato totalitario* by means of the party. For it was
stated in the fascist doctrine that: 'A party which
exercises total control over a nation is a new factor
in history.' To this extent it can be said that the
murder of the socialist deputy Matteotti, on 10
June 1924, served the purposes of the fascist regime,
despite the fact that it caused a serious political
crisis. For it was this political murder that enabled
the fascists to make substantial progress towards the

setting up of a totalitarian regime. For it led to the *coup d'état* and the dismissal of parliament, the passing of enabling acts on behalf of the head of government, the abolition of most civil liberties, the setting up of a special court, and the creation of political secret police, the *Organizzazione di Vigilanza e Repressione dell' Antifascismo*.

Certainly, the aim of establishing the *stato totalitario* was never realized in Italy, but it remained the aim and attempts were made to realize it. The fact that this attempt did not succeed was due to limitations imposed by geographical, economic and social conditions which have already been mentioned. Despite all their efforts, neither the National Socialists nor the Italian fascists managed to infiltrate the entire apparatus of the state and the army. In the Third Reich, the organs of the state and the party were in theory separate and even parallel, but in practice confused and conflicting. In fascist Italy, on the other hand, the party was itself a state organ. Corradini, the former nationalist, regarded this form of concentration of power, and the omnipotence of the state as the basic characteristic of Italian fascism. Thus Mussolini optimistically proclaimed that in the totalitarian state a nation would be ruled in a totalitarian fashion by the party. Because of the exclusivity of the one party system and the resulting privileged position of the party, it assumed an ecclesiastical character – irrespective of beliefs. The German translation of this concept which was formulated by Panuzio, *ecclesiasticità*, was, significantly, *bündischer Staat* (confederate state). An important disadvantage of this identification of state and party in Italy was that it prevented the party from fulfilling its first task, that of preserving and propagating the ideology. Even in Germany the party failed in this, despite the different structure, as is shown by the fact that, towards the end of the war, the Nazis appointed political commissars as *Nationalsozialistische-führungsoffiziere*, who were to be responsible for the political views of the soldiers. Nevertheless it is true to say that the parties in fascist Italy and in the Third Reich were, in comparison with other fascist systems such as Portugal, Spain and Poland, by far the most highly institutionalized.

After 1945 and under the influence of Stalin's period of rule in the Soviet Union there was a tendency to regard fascism exclusively as a totalitarian form of government, without any further distinction. Historiographers, who are now more concerned with sociological aspects, mostly reject this view today. However, it should be borne in mind that attempts at a comparative analysis of totalitarian forms of government, such as those in communist and fascist states, were undertaken long before the end of the last war. At the end of September 1923 Lloyd George pointed out that the anti-democratic movements in Europe had begun, not in Italy, but in Russia. According to this view, Lenin was the first fascist, in the sense that he was the first to replace the system of election by that of violence. Thus he referred to Dzerschinsky, who forced workers into service, as a 'fascist-communist'. When Luigi Sturzo undertook an analysis of Italian fascism in 1926, he too compared it with bolshevism. The difference between Italy and the Soviet Union was, in his view, that bolshevism was a communist dictatorship, or kind of left-wing fascism, and fascism was a conservative dictatorship or kind of right-wing bolshevism. In the same year, Francesco Nitti's book *Bolshevism, Fascism and Democracy* was published in German translation. Judged by the principles of parliamentary democracy, fascism and bolshevism seemed to him to be 'similar phenomena'. Both of them rejected the system of liberal democracy, and despite their differences, would feel drawn to each other. He saw fascism as a 'white bolshevism', a new reactionary force. In 1924 Torquato Nanni, although approaching the subject from a very different direction, described fascism and bolshevism as 'different, but not opposing episodes in the development of capitalism into socialism'. In 1948 Churchill, in his memoirs, called fascism the 'shadow or the spoilt child' of communism.

The exclusively totalitarian interpretation is no

longer held now. But the fact still remains that the totalitarian element in fascism, as in bolshevism, was an important factor, even though the motives for it were very different. This is demonstrated by the cult of violence in the Sorelian sense, and the concept of the elite and the significance of the mass basis for both systems. Thus Hugh Seton-Watson refers to fascism as a 'non-Marxist totalitarianism'.

The elements of totalitarianism in Italy consisted of the following: the single party with closed membership, that is, joining and leaving the party were not voluntary; a strictly hierarchical order, ruled from above, with the head of government directly controlled by the party secretary; control of the state youth organization and the corporations, which meant control of political opinion as well as leisure activity; total control of the economy by the syndicates; a system of spies in the professional or workers' associations, membership of which was compulsory; a party militia, run by the state, as a counter-balance to the monarchist army; total control of all mass media in order to manipulate public opinion. In fact, the party represented, in its hard core, 'a bulwark of ideological intransigence and extremism'.

Looking at these phenomena, one cannot deny that fascist Italy, although it was not wholly totalitarian, was clearly and consciously on the way to becoming a totalitarian state. This applied also to a greater or lesser extent to the other fascist, or 'fascistoid' regimes, like that in Hitler's Germany or Franco's Spain, where the state unity party, the *Falange tradicionalista y de las Juntas de Ofensiva Nacional-Sindicalista*, was formed at the end of 1936, in opposition to the Falange and the Monarchists.

Totalitarianism took on a particular form in Nazi Germany. The question of the relationship between the NSDAP and the state was never satisfactorily solved here, even though it was obviously of fundamental importance. The party remained in an ambiguous position, neither confined to the status of a subsidiary servant of the regime, nor elevated

Mussolini at the opening of the newly restored Julius Caesar Forum at Rome.

to that of an equal or superior authority. The pre-existent apparatus of the state was not paralleled by a corresponding party system – indeed, system was precisely what was lacking, for competences and responsibilities were distributed in a haphazard fashion, with few rigid demarcations and much overlapping. Thus the once fashionable description

Hitler conferring with his architect Speer, who later rose to become the highly effective overlord of German armament production.

'dual state' is not quite appropriate; the historian Martin Broszat has suggested instead the use of 'triple state' as a more exact concept, the third power being the authority of the charismatic *Führer*. Full authority derived from him alone, but his theoretical omnipotence was impeded in practice by the deficiencies of a structure that had evolved in such a confused way.

The one Nazi institution that was able to acquire a truly effective power base was the SS, under one of Hitler's most fanatical henchmen, Heinrich Himmler. The SS began life as a bodyguard and security unit; one of its main functions was to report on the party's internal security, a task which gave it an ideal position from which to build up its own

power. It was an elite troop, deriving its nominal power from the *Führer*; because it also absorbed the state police forces after 1933, the SS had in addition a strong substantive power base of immeasurable potential. Thus it became truly a state within a state, in the sense that it was its own normative authority, independent of the state's sovereignty; and although it was in theory Hitler's personal guard, it thus also had a built-in tendency towards total independence of status and action.

In line with the spirit of heroic nationalism which flourished in Germany after 1918 and regarded conflict as an end in itself, it was the life style of the SS and not its doctrine which was of fundamental importance. Theoretical principles were considered

Hitler greeting party members elected to the *Reichstag*. On his left are Dr Frick and Göring. On his right, Gregor Strasser and Stöhr. Behind Hitler sits Goebbels.

less important in the SS than in the NSDAP as a whole, or even in Italian fascism, in direct contrast to socialism and communism. But they did consider ideological teaching important, although this was confined to biology and history which could be manipulated for their own purposes. What Mussolini demanded of his fascists – faith, obedience, fighting – was what Hitler and Himmler desired above all of their SS men. Not the victory, but the fight itself was the crucial element. 'The essential thing is not what we are fighting for, but how we fight.' In the Nietzschean sense, they were aspiring to the impossible: it was the struggle itself that meant everything. Himmler, as early as 1941, was pondering how he could keep his SS men fresh after the victory. He would have them settle in the east as *Wehrbauern* (armed peasants) and do military duty by guarding the frontier.

Like all the fascist movements, the SS was ideologically backward-looking, but it combined its reactionary attitude with the principle of efficiency in military and civil action. In this the SS resembled the technocratic, managerial leaders of our own society. It was rightly remarked that this attitude on the part of the SS 'represented part of the spirit of our own time'. The SS was undoubtedly what the *Reichswehr* had unjustly been accused of being during the Weimar Republic, namely a state within a state. It rebuilt entire state organs for itself, and if the war had ended differently, would surely, in view of its will to power and the power it had acquired, have taken over leadership. After 1942–3 the SS aimed at divesting Hitler's racial and ideological war against the east of its ideological trappings, and at perfecting its content. In this endeavour it could not have been halted by Hitler or by 'loyal Heinrich'. The SS could not evade responsibility for the terrible crimes committed by their comrades at the orders of Hitler and Himmler, for they were the guards in the concentration camps. The collapse of the Third Reich put an end to the hopes of the SS of becoming the main power behind the state in its second era, whose form they had not yet

envisaged, and the slogan which they used towards
the end of the war – 'Everything we do is for the
Reich alone' – seemed somewhat unrealistic in view
of the number of foreigners within their own ranks.

*Hitler : der geniale Spiess-
bürger (Hitler – the brilliant
Philistine).*

FRANZ SCHAUWECKER

*Caesar – that is not so much
a man as a situation.*

LOUIS MADELIN

*If you want to deceive a people,
then flatter them shamelessly
and praise them ; you must first
serve them with words before
you can rule with words.*

FRIEDRICH GEORG JÜNGER, 1934

The Führerprinzip

When in 1927 Erwin von Beckerath examined the
development and nature of the fascist state, he found
that it was based on a *Spitzendiktatur* (a pointed
dictatorship) which penetrated the horizontal strata
of classes and united them with a clamp in the form
of the state power apparatus. To him it seemed that
the system was more important than the man, and
to this extent the structure of fascism seemed to him
to be far closer to that of bolshevism and the
absolutism of the seventeenth and eighteenth
centuries than to that of capitalism. He did admit,
however, that the ideological differences were vast.

Indeed, the ruling classes in the capitalist system
would surely have been satisfied if the fascists had
confined themselves to the task of taming the masses
of the working population, but this was prevented
by various important elements in fascism – its
ideology, its imperialistic nationalism, its extreme
racialism, and, above all, the charismatic personality
of the leader. Nor should it be forgotten that fascism
originated as an anti-bourgeois rebellion, not as the
saviour of bourgeois society. The significance of the
'leader' in all the fascist movements is evident. It

has nothing to do with the so-called *Königsdiktaturen* (royal dictatorships) which existed for a time in Jugoslavia, Spain and Bulgaria. For their legitimation derived from their monarchical nobility, and not from the capabilities and ambition of one individual who had no legal claim to power at all. But it is the appearance of a charismatic leader as the saviour of the despairing masses that is an essential feature of those fascist movements which achieved any political influence. This absolute, almost mystical relationship to the leader gave fascist movements a sectarian character and set them apart from normal parties, even when they took on the name of a party for tactical reasons.

The leader, when he and his movement had come to power, stood outside and above the state. Fascist doctrine and National Socialist state law, the development of which Hitler did not encourage, tried hard to give this situation a legal interpretation. This was bound to fail because the unique position of power that the fascist leader had acquired *vis à vis* the state could not be formulated in legal terms. It was possible only to describe it or circumscribe it. The legitimation of the leader was founded not on the power of the state but on that of his movement and his superior insight as the executor of the 'common will of the people'. Here a fine distinction was drawn between the opinion of the majority of the people – the German people, in this case – as shown by elections, and the 'true will of the people' as ascertained by the leader in a kind of mystic vision.

From a scientific point of view, the question of where to seek the immediate cause of fascism is irrelevant as well as insoluble, whether in the discontent of the masses or in the individual, charismatic power of the leader-figure. A crucial factor in fascist ideology was that the best should rule. It must also be borne in mind that many of the fascist leaders had previously belonged to large, often left-wing parties. This applied to Mussolini, Doriot, Quisling and Mosley. For many years Mosley had been active in the Labour Party. Doriot had for a long time been a leading member of the French Communist Party. Quisling had declared himself ready to build up the extreme left-wing Norwegian *Rote Garden*, before he founded his own fascist party. They had all, with the exception of Hitler, had thorough experience of the organization and life of political parties before their fascist period.

Thus, in the context of fascism and National Socialism one can speak of a 'democratic Caesarism', as Waldemar Gurian did in his book *Um des Reiches Zukunft* (1931). To this extent one can, like August Thalheimer, regard the Bonapartism of Napoleon III in a way as a predecessor of fascism in the twentieth century. Just as he became *Ersatzkaiser*, the substitute for Napoleon I, so Hitler became *Ersatzkaiser* in place of the Hohenzollerns for the Germans after 1918. In these fascist systems the party and the all-embracing state became as one. The party programme was submerged in the personality of the leader. Mussolini, like Hitler, carefully avoided tying himself down to any firm programme. This was made unnecessary by the leader's intuitive grasp of what the people wanted of him. Action always came first – it was interpreted and sanctioned afterwards. Thus fascism was by its very nature purely empirical and pragmatic, thereby differing essentially from other parties, even the conservatives.

Most of the fascist leaders were gifted demagogues and this, together with the fact that they almost always appealed to the people directly, making their spoken word far more important than their writings, has led to the personality of the leader becoming identified with the system itself. The name of the leader became a concept which evoked the whole system. By 1928 people were saying in Italy that there was no such thing as fascism, only 'Mussolinism'. Similarly people have spoken and still speak of Hitlerism, Francoism, of Maurrasism in Portugal, Pétainism, Gaullism, Salazarism, Nasserism, Perónism, McCarthyism and Poujadism.

However, this personification of a political system tends to divert attention from the fact that the fascist or 'fascistoid' leader was at best *primus inter pares* and never had power totally in his hands. He could never do entirely as he liked. The apparent power and omnipotence of the fascist leader was often enough severely limited in reality. Just as it is evidently wrong to see fascism as inherent in the national character of a people, it is also wrong to concentrate too much on the demonic nature of the pathological leader-figure when interpreting fascism.

The fascist leader had at best only symbolic value for the liberal bourgeoisie which felt threatened by socialism and communism. The Italian Prime Minister Giolitti despised fascism but wanted to use it as a weapon against communism. He hoped to be able to tame Mussolini and his movement, to civilize them. When Hitler had formed his government in 1933, a high officer in the *Reichswehr* asked a friend whether he believed that they had chosen the right 'great Manitou' to tame the discontented masses. Von Papen and the nationalist politicians like Hugenberg thought that they could call Hitler and his pack to heel like hounds they had set on to a deer but which were not allowed to injure it. In 1929 August Thalheimer, in his analysis of the political situation in Germany, wrote that a suitable dictator had not yet been found in the bourgeoisie but that if social and political conditions were right 'the most vulgar jingoist . . . would do'. The bourgeoisie and the army in the German Republic both believed that they needed such a 'lion-tamer and ring-master' who would tame the masses at the crack of his whip. They did not want to sully their own hands.

In the last analysis the leaders of the fascist movements in those states where they were able to come to power were merely participants in a power cartel. Wolfgang Schieder rightly points out that in future 'the central point in an analysis of fascism must be the politically compromising character of the fascist regimes'. In 1915 Corradini joined Mussolini's small band with his *Avanguardia* and invented the symbolic concept of the 'Duce'. In similar fashion all the fascist movements built up their 'leader' into their central figure. This theory of the personal

regime tends to obscure the fact of the system behind
it, which consisted of organizations struggling against
each other for power, while at the same time trying
to achieve a balance. To mention but one example,
the advisory commission of eighteen fascists on the
Italian constitutional reform of 1925 rejected 'the
institutions of an Imperial Chancellor, a Cardinal
Minister or Grand Vizir'. Mussolini had after all
often said to himself that the state must be an
'organized democracy' in which every citizen could
move freely. But this only applied to him and his
closest collaborators. Like Hitler he preferred the
Turkish system of government for his people. The
German *Gauleiter* and the Italian *ras* had considerable autonomy as long as they did not come into
conflict with the leader's intentions. It was all a
matter of, according to the Italian oath and all the
other fascist oaths, obeying the orders of the leader
without question and, if necessary, sacrificing one's
life for the fascist revolution.

The National Socialist Third Reich was no
totalitarian dictatorship in the sense of 'a monolithic,
authoritarian system inspired by a unified policy'.
Despite all the revolutionary slogans, the old social
order and the traditional ruling classes remained in
the fascist states. The conflicts between them and the
working class were simply petrified. In his study
Behemoth, which was published during the Third
Reich, Franz Neumann showed that the National
Socialist regime had not created a totalitarian state
but a form of direct rule over the suppressed masses,
which was without any rational legality and which
was dependent upon four largely autonomous groups,
each pressing its own administrative and legal
powers. These groups were the party, the army, the
bureaucracy and industry. If he had written his book
later, when more information became available, he
would have included a fifth group – the SS. In
Hungary under Horthy, there was a pluralistic
system of competing groups and organizations. As
in other fascist systems they formed an unstable
coalition, constantly warring with each other, but
without resorting to violence. Georges Sorel, in his

description of the intellectuals' occupation of the clubs during the French Revolution, referred to the 'multi-Caesarism' of the secret societies. So it was in the fascist regimes. But towering above all the fighting, rival groups was the symbolic figure of the *Führer* and Chancellor, the head of state and the leader of fascism who was not subject to any constitutional limitations. Instead of fulfilling the task of the head of government in a parliamentary democracy of smoothing out differences, here the leader played them off against each other. But no matter how important the authoritarian figure in fascism became, it must be borne in mind that this power position would never have been achieved without the interplay and conflicts between the various party organizations and social groups.

Fascism after 1945

*There must come a time when
there will be a science of
the future (as there is now
of the past).*

JOHANN GOTTFRIED HERDER, 1812

*Each of us is every man's
fascist.*

HANS MATHIAS KEPPLINGER, 1970

In 1958 Golo Mann asked whether National
Socialism represents a danger which is inherent in
twentieth-century democracy in general, not just in
Germany. Further, he asked whether the events
which led to 30 January 1933 were the result of
German history or were caused by international, by
world events. Since 1945 many historians, political
scientists and sociologists have devoted themselves
to the problem of whether fascism, at least in Europe,
was merely a unique phenomenon arising out of a
unique historical situation. In 1968 Seton-Watson
asked the 'tormenting question', whether fascism
has a future, or, in more concrete terms, 'which
social and political movements of the present day
or of the near future can be better understood in
view of our knowledge of fascism?'

Bardèche, who was a friend of a French fascist,
Brassilach, who was shot in 1945, expressed the
opinion after the war that fascism can only exist in
periods of crisis, and that only where there was a
spirit of angry heroism could there be possibilities of
development. In 1968 Mosley wrote that fascism
did not exist at the moment, not because an answer
had been found to it but because it belonged to the
era of the Second World War. In the same year,
S. J. Woolf expressed the opinion that the conditions
which might lead to a revitalization of fascism in a
totally different world situation did not exist. Anti-
communism had become common property through

The last fascist salute for Mussolini in the chapel of San Cissiano cemetery, Italy, where a burial service was held in 1957. The body of the *Duce* had only then been handed over to his widow, Rachele Mussolini, twelve years after his death.

the Cold War, imperialism had capitulated in the face of anti-colonialism, capitalism had proved itself after 1945, in contrast to the era before 1933, and international cooperation had improved enormously. Nevertheless, Woolf did not deny the possibility that a fascism of a quite different kind might arise to confront capitalism and democracy, developing perhaps from the ranks of the Churches, armies and the circles of radical left-wing intellectuals.

Trevor-Roper, on the other hand, agrees with Nolte that the era of fascism is over – only the uncritical dogmatists of the left still believe in it. Seton-Watson is not quite convinced – he agrees that there is no new fascism developing in Europe, but still sees a fascist hard core in certain radical nationalist movements. But he admits that most people in this age of affluence regard these groups as pathological relics from another age. Strong governments within democracy, like those of de Gaulle, Adenauer and de Gasperi, were generally regarded as the best means of preventing any rebirth of fascism. Iring Fetscher answers the question of whether the era of fascism is over with a conditional no. In his view a neo-fascism could develop if political elites were to mobilize latent elements in large sections of the population.

When considering the question of whether a 'new' kind of fascism could arise in the foreseeable future, one must also bear in mind that fascism, like any other political phenomenon, does not consist of consistent and unchanging features, but has its own history of development, and cannot be reduced to a static model. (The complexity and variability of fascism must, as we have already seen, be constantly borne in mind.) Alff, who must be regarded as representing the left-wing view, and who as a historian has studied Italian fascism, pointed out in 1970 that there were no more fascist parties anywhere, apart from the inevitable sects which cultivate the residue of fascism. Nolte has made similar remarks in his refutation of criticism of his well known thesis that the era of fascism was that of the two World Wars, and is therefore 'dead' now. He points out that he was referring to 'European national fascism'. Even something that is present can be dead.

After 1945, sociological and political interpretations of fascism developed in two directions. Either fascism and National Socialism were examined in isolation, without regard to fascism as a general phenomenon, or else all 'fascist' phenomena were included under the general category of totalitarianism. In the latter case fascism was used as a term for any kind of violence and dictatorship, and as Tasca and many others have done, to describe various forms of anti-fascism. Even Fetscher has to admit that fascism, National Socialism and communism, especially in its Russian form, show similar characteristics, such as one-party rule, the system of terror, censorship, the system of spies, and the militarization of the entire population and of youth in particular.

To avoid this dilemma, the radical left has coined a completely new system of political concepts which it uses very uncritically. The element of violence and suppression in fascism now becomes the repression of certain groups or classes of the population, or of whole peoples by the ruling classes. In their view the discontented masses, which were largely responsible for the rise of fascism, are becoming the frustrated masses which could provide the 'fascistoid potential' for a new fascism. At the moment, at least in Europe, fascism of the old kind does not exist; they call all national, nationalist and conservative movements in the western democracies 'fascistoid', using indiscriminately a term which has yet to be properly defined. Erwin K. Scheuch thus speaks of the 'resurrection of the redemptionist movements' which he sees both on the right and on the left. He defines the concept 'fascistoid' as used by the left as a 'term of denunciation used of any economic system not controlled by a communist party'. Thus any non-communist economic system is latently fascist.

There were also ideological and practical agreements between extremist groups of the left and right in the inter-war period from 1918 to 1933. Kurt Schumacher spoke once of 'red Nazis'. At that time, and today too, both political groups declared that the subjective interests of the minority represented the objective interests of the majority. In this sense both were elitist in their attitude. Because it is difficult to prove economic exploitation at the present time, the left has invented the concept of psychic exploitation, what Marcuse calls 'surplus repression'. They refer to right-wing anti-movements against social change as 'positions and repressions without rational justification'. In 1938 Ignazio Silone in his *School for Dictators* contrasted the primitive religion inherent in the 'new idolatry' of the fascists to the repressive system of modern production. Both sides believe in the chiliastic overcoming of man's alienation in the modern world of work, but with different ends in mind. Each side accuses the other of repression. Thus attacks are made on the hidden or, in Marcuse's phrase, 'institutional' means of repression in capitalist societies, such as the practical impossibility of operating a socialist daily press. Every limitation of the political freedom of a minority, no matter how small, is seen as a symptom of potential fascism. This had been clearly foreseen in 1936 by the former Italian communist Angelo Tasca. The communists saw everything as fascism – the state, the bourgeoisie, democracy, the Social Democrats. They would fight on all fronts. 'If everything is lumped together, the struggle becomes much simpler.' In 1970 the left-wing political economist E. Krippendorf claimed that the 'political class' of the USA was prepared to maintain the capitalist social structure of its country at the price not only of an inevitable 'escalation of repression' – namely the transformation of democracy – but at the price of the total annihilation of human life. Naturally he interprets the aid given by the United States to South America and southeast Asia as an instrument of repression applied by a conservative and imperialist ruling class. In his concept of this new fascism he includes repressive tolerance at one end of the pole and terrorist extremism at the other.

Both extremes, left and right, derive from the Romantic criticism of society which began with the start of industrialism and continued till the turn of the last century. Scheuch points out the similarity between the views of the National Bolsheviks in the Weimar Republic, the Italian fascists and the 'Extra-parliamentary opposition' in the Federal Republic, which applies even to details in the formulation of their views. The ruling class is accused of 'total manipulation'. Right- and left-wing terrorism is propagated to combat this, which, in the opinion of American radicals at Harvard could help 'to achieve understanding of transcendence'. Based entirely on the life philosophy on which fascism too was based they turned against rationality and advocated feelings, emotions and the free expression of the soul. Whether right- or left-wing, they wanted to participate in the 'service of revolution'. There are unmistakable spiritual links between right and left. The right-wing Hans Freyer formulated the concept of 'one-dimensional-man' long before the left-wing Marcuse. Nor can we ignore the influence of Carl Schmitt, the 'fascist' legal expert, on Jürgen Habermas. Left-wing, liberal political thinkers like Kurt Sontheimer may see the main danger as coming from the right, but they are also aware that on the

Metropolitan State University Library

left there is a tendency towards uncritical radicalization which brings them 'suspiciously close to
left-wing fascism'. The communist philosopher
Leszek Kolakowski called this tendency 'a caricature
of Nazism with Marxist phraseology'. Fear of
inadequacy leads, in the opinion of Günter Gaus,
to the desperate need to take refuge in a vague,
symbolic idea – such an idea is provided by the aim
of a world without conflict, a one-dimensional
society.

This has led people to gravely misjudge the
situation on the left, and to speak of the modern,
the new fascism. In the opinion of the chairman of
the Schleswig-Holstein Social Democrat Party,
Jochen Steffen, this is a factor created by the conditions posed by the Germany (Peace) Treaty. In his
view an actual danger for the parliamentary democratic society in the Federal Republic lies in the
ruling classes' exploitation of the existing 'socio-
technical system' of government.

In 1932 Fritz Sternberg analysed the sociological
structure of those sections of the German people
who were attracted by fascism; Fetscher has
attempted a similar kind of analysis after 1945. In
his view the fascist potential in the Federal Republic
lies, not in the 'old middle classes, but largely in the
new', in which he includes both white-collar and
blue-collar workers, whom the consumer society has
made into 'status-seeking pseudo-bourgeois'. This is
similar to the argument used by Lenin before 1914,
when he spoke of the 'workers' aristocracy'. Basically
they were less concerned with a rise in the social
position of the workers, than with the victory of the
elite represented by the Communist Party. Only to
this extent do they speak of their political opponents'
refascistization or fascistization.

In my discussion of the structural analysis of
fascism before 1939 I mentioned the lack of dif-
ferentiation shown by the communists. Certainly no
satisfactory answer has been given to the question
of how far fascism helped to maintain the position
of the bourgeoisie in Europe. This was very different
in the various geographical areas. The theory that

fascism was the last, extreme crisis within the bourgeois capitalist system has only very limited validity, and certainly did not apply to Germany in 1933. Thus the left in Germany are now trying to interpret the 'aligned society' of the Federal Republic as a new form of fascism. In the words of A. Görlitz it is an 'authoritarian society totally geared to production with the technocratic ideology of non-ideological objective compulsion'.

The indiscriminate and totally uncritical use of the term 'fascism' by left-wingers tempts them into applying it to every political idea that is opposed to their own, or to disown it entirely. According to Alff this term can only refer to the ideological superstructure of highly developed capitalism. But first, he says, one must analyse the psychic motives – only then can one use the term fascism. At the moment the term is being used in political journalism 'as an arbitrary term of abuse.' This, he says, could well be described as repression on the part of the left. The wide-spread abuse and misuse of the term is recognized by political scientists. Thus, like Lipset, one can only admit that there can be no firm prognoses concerning the development and direction of potential extremist political movements, such as those among the peasants and the miners. Therefore let us turn to the phenomenon of fascist parties or sects that have appeared since 1945.

The most interesting example in Europe is where fascism first originated and came to power – Italy. In 1970 Alff commented that fascism disappeared as quickly as it came to power. The decline of the *Movimento Sociale Italiano* (MSI), Italy's neo-fascist party, was, he wrote, inexorable, despite all its parliamentary efforts. The regional and municipal elections of 14 June 1971 seem, however, to contradict this view. The proportion gained by the MSI out of a total poll of 7,000,000 rose by 8·2 to 13·9 per cent. In Sicily the party received 390,000 votes, that is, 16·3 per cent. In Rome 258,000 people, that is 16·2 per cent, voted for the neo-fascist party. Very few of these voters were real fascists in the sense of belonging to the party, but merely dis-

Prince Valerio Borghese the instigator of the dilettante neo-fascist *coup d'état* of December 1971. The Prince, on the left, is accompanied by Giorgio Almirante and Franz Turchi, two high-ranking officials and deputies of the neo-fascist party *Movimento Sociale Italiano*.

satisfied and disorientated people. Because the MSI projected itself as the party standing for order, many people voted for it who condemned the widespread strikes and the growing crime rate in Italy. This represented the biggest shift to the right since 1953, when the movement received 5·8 per cent of the votes; after that the movement had suffered a sharp decline. Today it is skilfully exploiting all political and social tensions and problems in the country, to gain votes. Bearing in mind that in Sicily alone there are 300,000 unemployed and the Mafia is only inhibiting economic development, the growth of the popularity of the neo-fascist party is not surprising. Like Mussolini, the right-wing party says 'Basta emigrazione!' But the ordinary people believe that the parties and the Mafiose go fifty-fifty. 'The real Mafia is in Rome.' How closely left and right are linked in the minds of the voters is shown by the remark of a small tradesman from Messina: 'I am a Mao-fascist, of course.'

The possibilities of preventing a revival of fascism are as clear as they are limited – fundamental social reforms and a common anti-fascist front as there was after 1943. This year was a turning point for all the political movements. The anti-fascist parties began to think about those things they had in common which could perhaps have prevented fascism coming to power in 1922. The monarchists separated off from the neo-fascists. In 1957 they won 12 per cent of the votes in contrast to the 2 per cent of the neo-fascists. The first attempts to revive fascism began in 1946 when Guglielmo Giannini founded his *L'Uomo qualunque* (the common man) movement. In 1956 the right wing split off under the leadership of the former journalist, Giorgio Almirante, and founded the MSI. Their paper was given the truly fascist name of *Il Secolo d'Italia*. Like all other fascist movements in Europe, Almirante's group wanted to return to the origins of fascism, to the programme of 1919 and the radical manifesto of Verona, proclaimed in 1943. They constantly referred to the crisis in Italy's parliamentary democratic system and stressed that they stood for order and dignity. Almirante put an end to the decline suffered by his predecessors by shifting to the left in 1969. Today his movement has about 400,000 members, of whom 60,000 alone live in Rome. About 70,000 young people aged between fourteen and eighteen belong to the *Giovana Italiana*. Almirante also managed to instigate the return to the fold of thirteen right-wing, extremist and terrorist splinter groups, such as the *Ordine Nuovo*. He stands for an irrational anti-communism and his model is the Colonels' regime in Greece. He aims at a 'qualitative and selective democracy', and would like to set up a presidential government in the style of Adenauer or de Gaulle. His movement rejects any opening to the left and is doing its best to cultivate good relations with the army. Of course, neo-fascism in Italy will be no danger once a strong, democratic government succeeds in solving the social and economic problems of the country.

The situation in the German Federal Republic is considerably more complicated. While the economic

Italian neo-fascists being addressed by their leader, Giorgio Almirante, at a huge meeting in Rome's *Piazza del Popolo*, following their success in local government elections.

miracle prevented the wide-spread social discontent which would have been one of the motives for the rise of a new fascism, there was another motive – the deep, emotional resentment introduced into the political atmosphere of the country by those returning home, refugees and expellees and exiles. Even the best economic situation cannot eliminate this factor, and it has probably only been intensified by the *Ostpolitik* of the Social Democrat government.

In the period immediately following 1945, so-called 'post-fascism' was wide-spread among former, and still convinced National Socialists. With the disappearance of this generation from the political arena this has lost much of its significance. The predecessors of the NPD, the *Nationaldemokratische Partei Deutschlands*, which is today often regarded as fascist, were the *Deutsche Rechtspartei* of 1946, and the *Sozialistische Reichspartei* of 1949–52. These could be referred to as 'post-fascist', as today the NPD is regarded as representing a kind of neo-fascism or an 'adapted fascism'. It is generally agreed that the danger for western democracy lies not so much in the possibility of the rise of purely fascist parties, but rather in the infiltration of existing parties by nationalist, extreme right-wing or authoritarian groups. However, the enormous growth in the popularity of the NPD after 1964 has given rise to deep unease, both in Germany and abroad. As long as right wing radicalism only existed as sects, it was relatively uninteresting. In 1959 there were eighty-five organizations with 561,000 members, and in 1963 there were 123 organizations, but with only 24,000 members.

While these small sects merely served to enliven the statistics of the constitutional control office, the NPD was another matter altogether. In eighteen months, in seven provincial elections, it succeeded in winning the votes of 1,871,249 citizens, and 61 mandates to the *Land* assemblies. People became nervous and compared the situation with that of the NSDAP before 1930, before it had achieved its break-through, a situation which was called 'proto-

Otto Strasser at the foundation ceremony of his German Social Union Party in 1956. The Strassers (his brother Gregor was murdered in the 1934 Röhm putsch) were prominent leaders in the early days of the Nazi movement, but broke with Hitler when he failed to emphasize the party's socialist commitment as strongly as its nationalistic one. Otto escaped the *Führer*'s murderous vengeance, opposing from abroad the Hitler brand of National Socialism which he regarded as an obscene perversion of a still valid ideal.

Von Thadden, the then president of the *National-demokratische Partei Deutschlands* (NPD) at one of the party's election meetings. The NPD represented the last of several efforts to provide a political home and power base for the vast number of former Hitler supporters. These extreme nationalists, now disassociating themselves from the more outrageous excesses of the regime, scored remarkable election successes, several times during the fifties and sixties, on the local level.

fascist'. The left saw the rise of the NPD as inherent in the character of the Federal Republic, as an 'authoritarian democracy', thereby forgetting that this was the very thing, given economic stability, that would prevent any real breakthrough by the NPD. Admittedly, the programme of the NPD is partly conservative, partly genuinely reactionary. Its members want to create a counter-revolutionary movement to oppose the 'age of the masses', forgetting that National Socialism, which had similar aims, failed miserably. The two movements are similar in their 'anti' attitude towards many features of modern life. As far as anti-Semitism is concerned, the NPD treads very carefully, but then that has no relevance any longer in West Germany. Anti-Americanism is another matter – it can reckon with considerable support from extremists on the left

Violent confrontations between right and left-wing extremists in Paris.

and on the right. Certainly there are more than a few parallels with the ideology of the NSDAP. Of course the young people who advocate this 'fascism' do not want to be associated with Hitler in any way, but they are still a danger to parliamentary democracy. It is impossible to forecast the future of neofascism in West Germany.

In France too there were various 'fascistoid' movements after 1945. These included the dictatorial conservatism of General de Gaulle, with the *Rassemblement du Peuple Français*, Poujade's 'Populism', which won 2·5 million votes in 1956 because of its critical attitude towards the political parties; and finally the fascist interlude during the Algerian war, which led to a serious state crisis. Ultimately France overcame these dangers thanks to de Gaulle's strong government. In Great Britain these problems

Metropolitan State University
Library Services

did not arise. There fascism was dead after 1939.

Apart from the two former fascist powers, Italy and Germany, and excluding the two great western democracies, France and Britain, Europe still offers quite a wide range of regimes with fascist features. The Balkans and eastern central Europe can be counted out after 1945, because all the countries are in the hands of the communists, and fascist movements are only possible among the *émigré* groups abroad, such as the powerful, illegal and terrorist Ustasha movement among the exile Croats.

Many European systems of government have certain fascist features, but with great differences of quality and degree. Franco's Spain has its clerico-fascism, its single party decreed by the head of state, combining the monarchists with an unwilling Falange, and finally, the Catholic technocrats of the Opus Dei, God's militia, who largely run the state. Portugal, a Catholic, corporative state, is run by youngish technocrats under Caetano in the spirit of 'Salazarism' and the true, imperial spirit of Portugal. Convinced that it is the only state in Europe to understand the Third World, it spends 45 per cent of its national budget on the army, and keeps 125,000 soldiers in its colonies. It pays homage to the ideology of anti-colonial colonialism and the 'genuine world citizenship of a modern empire'.

The Colonels' regime in Greece, a descendant of the Metaxas dictatorship after 1918, is regarded by the European left as a 'dictatorship of terror'. It is in fact what Thalheimer once called an 'open dictatorship' – an armed militia, a right-wing, conservative unity party, close ties with the Church, and a large secret police. Some of the factors which led to the development of this dictatorship were the apparently revolutionary attitude of the Greek socialists (as in many other European countries) and the inadequacy of the monarchist conservatives. Experts refer to the 'Spaniardization' of the Greek question. Undoubtedly a military regime rules in Athens, but whether one can speak of terror in the fascist sense is an open question. In any case, a clear national and

social programme is lacking.

In Egypt a conspiratorial campaign against British rule began among young nationalist and socialist officers in 1939. They had hoped for help from the fascist powers, but this was in vain. The revolution of the officers on 23 July 1952 was directed against the corrupt monarchy and the reactionary priesthood. Their aim was to achieve a democratic people's community, a republic and a powerful army. The officers of the Revolutionary Council wanted to restore the unity of the Egyptian people – in so far one can speak of a nationalistic dictatorship, but hardly of a fascist regime.

So much for Europe. Literature ascribing fascist tendencies to the United States, and above all to her ruling class, is growing steadily. In 1937 Robert A. Brady offered several examples of the fascist attitude of certain American businessmen. In his opinion, if a situation arose in the United States

December, 1967 and the three men who imposed dictatorial military government in Greece. Left to right: General Zoitakis, Regent; Brigadier S. Pattacos, Deputy Prime Minister and Minister of the Interior; and Colonel G. Papadopoulos, the Prime Minister.

206

Neguib and Nasser, the leaders of the 1952 officers' *coup d'état* which overthrew Egypt's monarchy and the ineffectual and corrupt King Farouk. Nasser, associated in the thirties with the Egyptian fascist 'green shirts', was politically the infinitely more astute and dynamic of the two. He soon ousted Neguib and in 1954 became President of Egypt. His determination to improve the country's economic and military status, to wipe out the humiliating military defeat inflicted by Israel during her war of independence and to achieve greatness, made him immensely popular among the Arab masses and in a broader context, also made him a spokesman for all Third World aspirations. True to his populist and vaguely fascist ideals, he broke the power of the former ruling classes by his land reform and nationalization measures, but opposed and on ocassions, brutally supressed, communism. Increasing dependence on Russian military and economic support notwithstanding, he remained firmly convinced that in his one-party state, the Arab Socialist Union would discover its own, indigenous, non-Marxist road to socialism.

similar to that in Germany in 1933, there would be the same racial terrorization, this time directed at Negroes, Jews, Mexicans and Japanese. Though people today accuse the USA of being a 'militaristic and aggressive' nation, it is another question whether the basically very conservative attitude underlying the idea of the *Pax Americana* is really a fascist one. Is it not that her basically isolationist attitude in two World Wars and towards her great communist rival, has been manœuvred, in the interests of self defence, into actual aggression, by circumstances and also by the ruling class?

It must also be borne in mind that in the United States in the nineteenth and early twentieth century, there were many popular movements which supported the small, decent man against Congress, political parties, big industry and other powers, demanding direct democracy with the right to petition, and the use of the referendum. People often forget that American democracy was always violent. The strong sense of community remained alive, with its rejection of 'foreign' elements. This is the only way to understand the McCarthy witch hunts after 1945. In the thirties there had been fascist movements in America which attacked the Jews and the power of the big financiers, and whose supporters numbered several millions. The great populist leader Governor Huey Long, who was murdered in 1936, wanted to save the middle classes from the upper classes, with very dictatorial means.

Today there are fascist tendencies on the left as well as on the right. Bearing in mind the tendency to violence that is already there, it is a worrying fact that there are 90,000,000 fire-arms in private hands in the United States. In view of the national humiliation suffered by the Americans in Korea and Vietnam, left-wing radicals are speaking of a potentially fascist reaction of right-wing groups resulting from their frustration at these national setbacks. One must not forget either the radicalism of the left-wing 'sub-culture'. When the Rolling Stones gave their huge concert in Altamont in

Overleaf: A crowd of New York workers gathered outside New York's City Hall to demonstrate in favour of President Nixon's policy in South-East Asia.

Below: Barry Goldwater, the defeated Republican contender in the 1964 American presidential election. An advocate for stiffer resistance to communism and Negro advancement, he alienated the more progressive voters in his own party, thus contributing to President Johnson's overwhelming victory.

President and Eva Péron. General Péron, although installed as President of Argentina by the army, owed his power to his popularity with the dispossessed urban proleteriat. His *Justicialismo*, basically a fascist concept, aimed at achieving national greatness and social justice without drastically interfering with the existing order. Aided by his flamboyant wife, he introduced social and welfare legislation. But deepening economic crises and an increasingly dictatorial style of government led to his overthrow by the antagonized middle classes and the Church.

California they hired three hundred Hell's Angels as security guards. They were stylized as the opponents of the ruling social class but the result was brutal violence and a murder. The Angels wear the swastika as a symbol of their rejection of common standards of decency and their rejection of 'civilized' morality; some admire Hitler as a man of action in the same way. In the opinion of one communard 'the Angels have shown themselves to be greater fascists than the establishment pigs'. But here too, a serious economic crisis would be necessary before the possibilities of latent fascism on either the left or the right became visible.

Wolf Grabendorff defined the situation in South America in the following way: 'How can states be ruled which will not allow themselves to be ruled?' The economies of the subcontinent are so unstable and their structure so feudalistic that such difficulties are not surprising. Opposing Castroism in the 'development dictatorship' in Cuba is the *Führer-*

prinzip of the South American military dictatorships, the supporters of 'Caudillism' with their opponents, the left-wing guerrillas. With astonishing liberality, left-wingers even refer to Cuba as the 'development dictatorship of the free world'.

The nearest thing to a fascist experiment in South America was in Argentina from 1943 to 1955 under President Juan Perón, who was responsible for 'Perónism', or the 'fascism of the lower classes'. Perón would never have achieved power without the support of the poor and the trade unions. He admired Hitler and Mussolini and believed in the concept of the powerful state, but he was against the corruption of the parties and the politicians, and wanted to protect the interests of the workers. The bourgeois middle class was against him. But the workers elected him, not the socialists. He only fell when the Church and the army turned against him.

The first South American development dictatorship was the *Estado Novo* of President Vargas in Brazil. His dictatorship, which lasted from 1930 to 1945, was a 'democracy with strong muscles', based on nationalism and socialism; it was a government of strict but just leaders. His supporters were the integralists or green-shirts, similar to Perón's 'shirtless ones'. He came to grief because of his oil policy, which was directed against the United States.

Purging Indonesia of communists. President Sukarno's aggressive foreign policies and the growing poverty caused by his military confrontations with the Dutch and Malaysians, as well as his increasing reliance on communist support, alienated the army on whose co-operation his rule ultimately rested. A communist uprising culminating in the execution of several generals gave the army an opportunity to strike back. Curtailing President Sukarno's powers before replacing him with General Suharto, the army launched an anti-communist campaign in the course of which more than a million people are believed to have been killed.

Vargas once declared that 'my party is the military'. In South America the armed forces have great political influence. It must also be borne in mind that they by no means always represent reactionary forces. Interests overlap here in many ways. Certainly the *coup d'état* in South America has almost become accepted as a legitimate political manœuvre. Since 1930 there have been fifty successful army putsches. But it must be stressed that in some states the military is by no means reactionary, and is aiming at the technocracy of social revolution, with its *acción cívica*. This happened in Bolivia, Venezuela, Colombia and Peru, thus giving rise to the expression, the 'Peruvian sickness'. The military, which in the USA is trained to consolidate the infrastructure, in these countries stands for social reform and nationalism. References have been made to 'Nasserism' in relation to Peru, but regimes are not necessarily fascist because they have no mass basis of support.

Nor can one apply this term to the regimes in south and east Asia – they are mostly authoritarian, anti-democratic military regimes such as in Pakistan, Indonesia, South Vietnam and South Korea. These states are inherently suspicious of parliamentary democracy because they suffered oppression under the imperialism of western democracies. In all these states the army is the crucial factor determining political power. Even in China Chou En-lai declared 'we are one with the army'. Although Mao has stated that the party must control weapons, the army is of crucial importance. These regimes, which are often in newly independent states, are military dictatorships using partially terrorist methods, but it would certainly be wrong to call them fascist states. They are almost all of them 'development dictatorships' with a reactionary or progressive political structure, although these characteristics are often enough varied even within one country. The question of the possibility of a later fascist development must remain open.

No serious historian has yet attempted to give a final
judgement about fascism. The future lies in darkness. No one can attempt to answer 'the bold
question of fate', whether fascism has a future and
if so, how this could be confronted. The solutions
which have been offered on many sides and by many
political movements can only be partial and superficial.

One thing seems certain however – most analyses
hardly go beyond a moral condemnation of brutality
and terrorism, although these have always existed
throughout the history of mankind, and have not
shattered men's belief in humanitarian progress.
In the era of the World Wars, in which we are still
living, the use of terror and violence has grown
appallingly. Attempts to make comparative historical
examinations of these phenomena – to see fascism,
that is, in every previous violent or totalitarian
episode – risk reducing disparate movements to a
single all-embracing category which distorts and
disguises the material differences between them.
The value of investigations of this kind lies precisely
in their capacity to identify the distinguishing marks
of superficially similar phenomena. If they fail to do
this, they merely obscure the potential for preventing
the re-emergence of one or other of these diverse
political movements. On the other hand, one
cannot accept the communist habit of drawing a fine
distinction between the horrors perpetrated by the
fascists, and those committed during the purges of
Stalin and Mao, which also caused the deaths of
millions. One cannot accept this double standard,
nor can one accept the attitude of the NPD in West
Germany, which totally denies the responsibility of
the German people for the mass murders committed
under the Nazis, as does the communist government
of East Germany. Both attitudes are historically
and morally untenable.

But the mass terror and the mass murders are,
however terrible this may sound, only concomitants
of those systems. The essence of fascism lay in its
attempt to breed a new type of human being which
inevitably resulted in the desire to exterminate the

Conclusion

'counter-image'. The development of man went from the man of ancient times, influenced by Christianity and humanism, via the political man of the eighteenth and nineteenth centuries, to the 'natural' man of the twentieth century, who was an easy prey to fascism because he was so easily manipulated. But the dark urge that this new human type had for strong leadership remained unfulfilled and was finally bitterly disappointed.

In the fascist states there was a vast, yawning gulf between this projected image of man and the actual practice of fascist education. For the image needed decades, if not centuries, of quiet, steady work, and fascism, with its life philosophy of constant action, was committed to constant change. The human image at least was idealistic, in contrast to the actual training and leadership which was totally pragmatic, cynical and immoral. It was in this that fascism decisively failed in the past.

Turning to the present and the future, the following theories are possible:

1. The era of fascism is definitely over. Those 'post-fascist' sects and organizations which still exist have only traditional value, and no political significance. This is Ernst Nolte's theory.

2. Applying the saying 'Each of us is every man's fascist', one sees in even the slightest national or conservative tendency the beginnings of a 'fascistoid' attitude which must be fought in the interests of progress and radical socialism. This is roughly the attitude of the extreme left and the left-wing intellectuals in the USA, France and West Germany, and in many other countries in Europe and overseas.

3. New, completely different forms of fascism are possible. I have discussed this theory at the beginning of the chapter concerning post-war fascism. Mosley's concept of Europe belongs in this category.

4. In modern, industrial society, particularly in Europe, fascism is no longer necessary, because other more harmless means of political repression are available.

Mirgeler refers to the modern state as an 'objectified, functioning apparatus'. In 1965 James H. Meisel

commented in his study of Pareto and Mosca that
fascism had become superfluous since people had
become more disciplined and politically apathetic
and resigned themselves to regimes which remained
democratic in form. He called this form of government 'managerial democracy'. In West Germany at
the present time the left tends to use the term
'technocratic fascism' to describe the political side
of 'totalitarian industrialism'. Certainly the Marxist
theory of men's alienation in industrial society is
relevant here, but it still does not explain why one
should regard this expression of the human urge for
organization as fascism.

Here we should take a brief look at *planisme* in
France. In 1961 Maurice Bardèche wrote in his
book *Qu'est-ce que le fascisme?* that the essence of
fascism was not determined by the absolute rule of
one man, nor by biological racialism, intolerance,
persecution of the Jews or by the secret police, but
solely by the 'spirit of an elite'. This spirit opposed
the uncommittedness of democracy and the domination of pleasure-seeking egoists, in order to achieve
true socialism on the basis of the first fascist programme. In his view this new fascism was in favour of
national independence within a united Europe, was
anti-communist and authoritarian. It did not rely on
the people, the 'masses'. Its model was not Fidel
Castro but José Antonio Primo de Rivera and Nasser.
In his view the Gaullist movement would have been
fascist if it had not had de Gaulle as its leader.

But it was under de Gaulle, and later under Pierre
Mendès-France, that the technocrats came to power
in France. Their programme was based on the *Plan
du 9 Juillet 1934*, which had an introduction by the
writer Jules Romain. This elite of young radicals
or 'Young Turks' was opposed to the rigidity of
traditional forms of parliamentary democracy in
France. It wanted to replace the policies which
were dictated by petty, egoistical interests by the
discovery and realization of the 'objective necessities'
of modern society. It wanted to strengthen the
power of the executive and to establish strong,
economically self-sufficient regions. These planners,

who were called by their opponents technocrats and 'synarchists', did not want a hegemony of pure technicians, but one run by administrative experts who would make their decisions not on party political grounds but according to purely objective considerations. 'The technocratic impulse and the technocratic judgement are among the crucial factors of our time.'

The fact that these technocrats seem to be totally politically uncommitted worries many people. Fetscher sees in the abstract, objective power drive of the technocrats a danger of 'fascistization'. However, the new left recognizes that 'under the changed conditions fascism in its old form will not come back again, because it has become superfluous as an instrument of power'.

I have dealt with fascism as a political phenomenon and as one belonging to a particular era. The questions concerning its possible further existence or non-existence have been put, but cannot be answered definitively. If this study has served any practical purpose, I hope that it will have helped to clarify certain concepts and therefore to make the political phenomenon of fascism, its origins, its effect and its disappearance, more comprehensible.

Bibliography

ABENDROTH, WOLFGANG, ed., *Faschismus und Kapitalismus: Theorien über die sozialen Ursprünge und die Funktionen des Faschismus* (Frankfurt, 1967)

ARENDT, HANNAH, *The Origins of Totalitarianism* (London, 1958)

BECKERATH, ERWIN VON, *Fascism,* in *Encyclopaedia of the Social Sciences, vol. 5* (New York, 1949)

CARSTEN, F. L., *The Rise of Fascism* (London, 1967)

CHABOD, F., *The History of Italian Fascism* (Chester Springs, 1963)

CORNELL, JULIEN, *The Trial of Ezra Pound* (London, 1966)

COTTER, C. P., *Fascism,* in *A Dictionary of the Social Sciences,* ed. Julius Gould and W. L. Kolb (New York, 1964)

GASMAN, DANIEL, *The Scientific Origins of National Socialism* (London, 1971)

GIRARDET, RAOUL, *La Société militaire dans la France contemporaine, 1815–1939* (Paris, 1953)

GULICK, CHARLES, *Austria from Habsburg to Hitler* (Cambridge, 1948)

HARRISON, JOHN, *The Reactionaries: W. B. Yeats, Wyndham Lewis, Ezra Pound, T. S. Eliot, D. H. Lawrence* (London, 1967)

HAYES, PAUL M., *Quisling: The Career and Political Ideas of Vidkun Quisling, 1887–1945* (Newton Abbot, 1971)

HEIST, WALTER, *Genet und andere: Exkurse über faschistiche Literatur von Rang* (Hamburg, 1965)

HELLER, HERMANN, *Europa und der Faschismus* (Berlin and Leipzig, 1931)

Journal of Contemporary Fascism, vol. 1 (1966), *No. 1, International Fascism: 1920–1945*

KEREKES, LAJOS, *Abenddämmerung einer Demokratie: Mussolini, Gömbös und die Heimwehr* (Vienna, 1966)

KEREKES, LAJOS, ed., *Allianz Hitler-Horthy-Mussolini: Dokumente zur ungarischen Aussenpolitik 1933–1944* (Budapest, 1966)

KIRKPATRICK, IVONE, *Mussolini, study of a demagogue* (London, 1964)

KNICKERBOCKER, H. R., *German Crises* (New York, 1932)

LANDAUER, CARL and HONEGGER, HANS, *Internationaler Faschismus* (Karlsruhe, 1928)

MEISEL, JAMES, *Pareto and Mosca* (Englewood Cliffs, 1965)

METTLER, C., *Józef Pilsudski* (Fribourg, 1938)

MOHLER, ARMIN, *Die konservative Revolution in Deutschland 1918–1932* (Darmstadt, 1972)

MOSLEY, OSWALD, *My Life* (London, 1968)

NAGY-TALAVERA, NICHOLAS M., *The Green Shirts and the Others: A History of Fascism in Hungary and Rumania* (Stanford, 1970)

NOLTE, ERNST, *Three Faces of Fascism* (London, 1965) *Der Faschismus von Mussolini zu Hitler. Texte, Bilder und Dokumente* (Munich, 1968)

PAYNE, S. G., *Falange* (Stanford, 1962)

PSICHARI, ERNEST, *L'Appel des Armes* (Paris, 1945)

REMOND, RENÉ, *The Right Wing in France: From 1815 to de Gaulle* (Pennsylvania, 1966)

ROBINSON, RICHARD A. H., *The Origins of Franco's Spain: The Right, the Republic and Revolution, 1931–1936* (Newton Abbot, 1970)

SCHOENBAUM, DAVID, *Hitler's Social Revolution: Class and Status in Nazi Germany 1933–1939* (London, 1967)

SHEPHERD, GORDON, *Engelbert Dollfuss* (London, 1961)

SMITH, BRADLEY F., *Heinrich Himmler: A Nazi in the Making 1900–1926* (Stanford, 1971)

STEIN, GEORGE H., *The Waffen-SS: Hitler's Elite Guard at War 1939–1945* (Cornell, 1966)

STERN, FRITZ, *The Politics of Cultural Despair* (London, 1961)

SZINAI, MIKLÓS and SZÜCS, LÁSZLÓ, eds., *The Confidential Papers of Admiral Horthy* (Budapest, 1965)

TASCA, ANGELO, *The Rise of Italian Fascism 1918–1922* (New York, 1966)

TOURNOUX, J. R., *Pétain et de Gaulle* (Paris, 1966)

WEBER, EUGEN, *Varieties of Fascism* (Princeton, 1964)

WOOLF, S. J., ed., *The Nature of Fascism* (London, 1968)

WOOLF, S. J., ed., *European Fascism* (London, 1970)

Metropolitan State University
Library Serv
St. Paul, MN 55108

Acknowledgements

The photographs in this book are reproduced by kind permission of the following:
Bilderdienst Süddeutscher Verlag: 14, 17, 20, 21, 22, 23, 26, 34, 36, 46, 50, 51, 52, 53, 61, 63, 79, 85, 87, 94–5, 107, 108, 109, 110, 115, 117, 119, 120, 121, 124, 128, 129, 153, 157, 162, 183, 206, 210.
Keystone Press: 10, 12, 13, 15, 18, 19, 25, 29, 32–3, 39, 40, 41, 49, 58, 60, 65, 74, 75, 76, 84, 123, 127, 136–7, 138, 139, 140, 150, 164, 181, 192, 198, 200, 201, 202, 203, 205, 207, 208–9.
Private Archives of Dr. Guenther Deschner, Gütersloh, Germany: 2–3, 4–5, 18, 27, 31, 37, 44, 48, 55, 68, 69, 70, 71, 84, 89, 90, 92, 130, 159, 173, 175, 211.

The illustrations for this book come from several sources. If we have unintentionally infringed copyright in any illustration reproduced in this book, we offer our apologies and, upon being satisfied as to ownership of the copyright, we will be happy to pay the reproduction fee.

Index

ST. PAUL
D
726.5
.S38
1973